# Duke's
## CHOWDER HOUSE

# AS WILD AS IT GETS

## Duke's Secret Sustainable Seafood Recipes

### Including Intimate Tales of the Legend Himself

# AS WILD AS IT GETS

## Duke's Secret
## Sustainable Seafood Recipes

### Including Intimate Tales of the Legend Himself

# DUKE MOSCRIP &
## CHEF "WILD" BILL RANNIGER

Principal Photography
### Ingrid Pape-Sheldon

AVIVA
PUBLISHING
New York

Address all inquiries to:  Duke's Chowder House
7858 Green Lake Drive N.   Seattle, WA 98103
(206) 283 8422 ext 4   |   www.DukesChowderHouse.com

Published by: Aviva Publishing, Lake Placid, NY
(518) 523-1320  |  www.AvivaPubs.com

ISBN: 978-1-9431643-2-5
Library of Congress: 2015915847

Producer/Art Director: Bettina Carey
Principal Photography: Ingrid Pape-Sheldon
Chief Editor: Amy Waeschle
Copy Editors: Seth Godwin and Tyler Tichelaar
Design Director: Aileen Yost
Designer: Suzanne Harkness

First Edition
Printed in the United States of America
Every attempt has been made to properly source all material.

# Contents

"Remember, wherever your heart is,
that's where you will find your treasure."
— Paolo Coehlo

This book is dedicated to my children,
my grandchildren, and my
grandchildren's grandchildren.
That is where my heart is.

# Unforgettable, That's What You Are

When I first got into the restaurant business in 1972 I only did so as an investor, or so I thought. I had no idea that what started out as an investment in one restaurant would in time turn into my life's work and before I knew it nearly forty years of living my dream would pass right before my very eyes.

For the last several years I have often wished that I had put down into words the many stories that have been woven into the fabric of Duke's Chowder House, as well as to include the many tasty recipes that have been inspired by my quest to serve the best food on the planet. But year after year would go by without the time to do so. When I finally came to the conclusion that the time was now a lot of things fell into place.

It all started when I was approached by our Marketing Director, Bettina Carey, with a question. She asked, "Have you ever wanted to write a cookbook?" Well, "What a coincidence," I said. So, the journey began to produce our long awaited cookbook.

At the center of this whole project was Bettina, the leader of the pack, aka producer/art director/food stylist... the list of her hats grows daily. Together she and other very talented people drove me and the project beyond my own known limits. She held the vision to its fruition, guiding each and every detail. Her enthusiasm and joy is what brought this project to completion. She navigated the ship, herded cats at times, and reminded us of what was needed to be done every step of the way. Without her determination and guidance the project would not have been successful.

Our photographer, Ingrid Pape-Sheldon worked tirelessly on our images, but more importantly, she filled the book with amazing colorful photos of our dishes and her wonderful personality made our food styling so much fun. Her famous line became, "oh just one more," which usually meant dozens more photos that resulted in some of our best shots. The result is that we have stunning images that are often the most real photos of us having a good time. Her husband and business partner, Frank Sheldon also held the fort together several times when Ingrid was traveling.

Many other talented photographers and illustrators provided other photographs and memorabilia that make this book really fun to read. We want to acknowledge them each individually. Their names are on the second copyright page along with the page number of their photo(s) or illustration(s). Georgio Brown, Roddy Scheer and Rich Carr deserve special recognition for having accompanied me during my Pacific Northwest and Alaska adventures shooting videos and photos, a few photos from each have been included in this book. Thank you all for braving the sea with me.

Aileen Yost, our chief graphic designer, whom we have worked with for many years now, continues to delight us with her instinctive knowledge of just what best represents our brand, as if she was living right in our mind. She introduced us to Suzanne Harkness, an InDesign expert who came into the project during a critical time. Together they had the right expertise and talent to expeditiously lay out the images and stories in such a way that we can all be proud of their efforts for many, many years to come.

Of course it goes without saying that we got a great deal of benefit by working with Patrick Snow, our book coach, who guided us with his expert coaching. Along the way we got to work with his fiancé, Nicole Gabriel who started our technical book layout process. As well, he introduced us to Susan Friedmann of Aviva Publishing who made our publishing process possible. All are great beings!

I am also really grateful to have had the opportunity to work with my daughter, Amy Waeschle, who was the chief editor in charge of what has turned out to be more than 380 pages of content. It was such a special time for us to sit side by side at times going over every single recipe and to have her bring her expertise as both an author herself and a professional editor to the project. Our other editors included Seth Godwin and Tyler Tichelaar. Together each combed over every word to ensure that our stories were accurate, were told with meaning and often times funny.

Dr. Bradford Weeks was the perfect person in my life to provide some additional knowledge for your benefit and ours regarding healthier choices and I cannot thank him enough personally for his help to keep me fit and feeling healthy. He and his wife, Laura, helped Bettina and I come up with some very playful names to our recipes. We hope you will see humor in the names.

Our fishermen, fisherwomen and many of our vendors have supported us for years and deserve a lion's share of thanks for making this book possible. You can see a full listing of our DukeWorthy™ providers in our copyright page and the names of several of our fisher people in the pages that feature them. Their sustainable practices help make our food taste sooo good!

Bob Bracht, our print expert with Colorgraphics, ensured that each turn of the page would give you pause to see and feel the magic that we hope will also delight your palate. He was always available when we called upon him and has such a bright disposition which made the printing process pleasant and fun.

Of course, this cookbook would not be possible without "Wild" Bill Ranniger, our Executive Chef. Bill and I are known as the "Food Dudes" for our constant dedication and co-creation of tasty dishes for over 21 years together. "Wild" Bill makes food ideas come to life. He has also been a calm and steady force in training and developing our chefs at our six locations. He has been along my side all these years to bring you the best tasting seafood on the planet. He of course has become a longtime friend in the meantime. Together with all our chefs (as seen on pg 26), "Wild" Bill has made Duke's a force to be reckoned with in any food competition.

A special thank you goes to my son, confidant and business partner, John Moscrip. As I write later in the book, John has not only enriched my life, he has improved the operation of our company in a big way. He, along with John Thelen, our Director of Operations, Kristina Dixon, our CFO, Marie Dominguez, our Administrative Manager as well as our entire team kept Duke's running and all helped me stay on time for every meeting. (Hardy har har…they will know why I laugh.) Many of you are featured in the pages of this book and we are honored to have included some of your shining faces.

Last but certainly not least, I want to thank my entire family, including my new bride Cybele (who is the light of my life) and chefs Lauren Waeschle, Elsa Waeschle, Hannah Moscrip and Hudson Moscrip, my grandkids. Each possesses a creative spirit and delightful personality that surely is sweeter than all of the desserts put together.

And to you, our valued guest and now cookbook reader, we could not have completed this book without believing that each and every one of you would read it and delight in recreating our recipes in your own home but enjoy reading our story, too.

Thank you one and all!

Sustainably yours,

# The Best Tasting Seafood On The Planet

This book is all about taste and flavor. It is what we strive for in every recipe. I know, I know. Everyone talks about flavor, but few recipes really have "outstanding" flavor, the kind that makes you go "Wow!" We have worked on these recipes for years to make them better and better, sometimes tweaking the same recipe over and over, trying different sauces, altering the ingredients, changing the amount of each ingredient to get it just right. Unusual combinations like Duke blueberries and Laura Chenel goat cheese with Wild Alaska Salmon deliver something special. What's Up Wasabi Aioli makes our quesadillas (and just about everything else) taste spectacular. No bland food here. Crushed macadamia nuts with Alaska Halibut combine with a hazelnut syrup and beurre blanc to give you an old-fashioned butterscotch flavor you cannot find anywhere. This is what we strive for and what you can discover in our recipes. I encourage you to go on a Duke Flavor Adventure and cook these recipes for your family and friends. I guarantee they won't have experienced them anywhere else but your kitchen and ours.

Now, I must add that even though the flavor of our recipes is truly spectacular, it is enhanced because of our sourcing and the superior processing of the fish at the source. The best-tasting seafood on the planet requires the best sourcing. You will discover in these pages the ongoing pursuit of exemplary seafood capture and processing. DukeWorthy™ is a term we use to describe our expectations for superior sourcing and fish handling. DukeWorthy™ food tastes better because we've ensured its freshness and outstanding quality. You will also notice that the names of all our seafood is capitalized along with the word "Wild." We think Wild Seafood deserves special treatment. You will also see that we capitalize the word "Chowder." It, too, deserves special treatment. After all, it did win the Seattle Chowder Cook-Off an unprecedented three years in a row.

Additionally, all our food is sustainable. This doesn't necessarily make the food taste better. It just ensures that my grandchildren and yours will have something tasty to eat. And, it's the right thing to do. Take care of the planet. It's the only one we have.

So, here's to flavor. Let it reign.

*"It's sooo good"*

# It's All About
# The People . . .

Extraordinary
beyond any doubt.

# The Food Dudes —

## A Brotherhood Bound In Mutual Respect And Flavor

To call Duke's Executive Chef "Wild" Bill Ranniger a brother is an understatement. We have worked together for more than twenty years and Duke's would not be what it is without my trusted friend "Wild" Bill. No matter what crazy food scheme one of us dreams up, "Wild" Bill is always there to make it work or know when it's time to pull the plug.

I remember one instance of the "Leaning Tower Of Seafood." "Wild" Bill had this great idea of stacking delicious seafood on a huge skewer and serving it as our little tribute to Italy. The only problem was that our leaning towers didn't just lean; they toppled.

We had to pull the plug until one summer day when the solution to our structural tower issues came in the form of a watermelon. With a nice base of sweet summer melon, the tower didn't topple and our tribute to Italy made a summer comeback. As a bonus, it turns out that juicy watermelon and seafood are delicious together in a summer appetizer.

We call ourselves the "Food Dudes," and this moniker has led us on some delicious adventures, from our Silky Sensual Pan Seared Wild Alaska Salmon with Beurre Blanc Sauce, (one of our most popular and complex dishes) to our Award Winning Chowders. Bill and I have countless hours of dedication in making each and every dish the best. It is rare to have such a lasting connection and collaboration with another person. Bill and I just "get" each other, and it has been an honor to build Duke's with him. Here's to you, "Wild" Bill, and to many more food adventures that bring only the best flavors to our guests.

# My Son John,
# Business Partner And Friend

As a parent, you want the best for your children; you lay the foundation and values for their futures and hope they thrive in the world at least in part because of it. It has been an honor watching my son grow up and become such a wonderful and amazing person. John has not only enriched my life and his own family, he has also improved the operation of our company in a big way. I am so proud to call him my son, business partner and friend.

John has been around Duke's his entire life from bussing and waiting tables to bartending and training to be a cook. I have always admired how he took on every task with amazing dedication and vigor. When he became my partner in 2005, I had been overseeing operations by myself at Duke's since 1976 when we first started. After all those years, it was time to get some help.

I always knew John would be something great. People have been drawn to him his entire life. He is just a natural with people and has more best friends than I can count. This is a natural skill that is inherent in great leaders, and John is one of the best I've ever seen. This charisma gives him the innate ability to get people to do what he wants while making them feel great about it.

John and I make a great team, and this change has made Duke's truly great. John is much different from me. We complement each other like few father-son duos. We challenge each other, and when the dust settles from each challenge, Duke's continues to prosper. I am humbled and proud to see my son thrive with me as we make great efforts to take care of everyone who crosses our path.

———————————— ♦ ————————————

"I never imagined how rewarding it would be to work with my dad. I have learned so many lessons about life, business and personal relationships because of my time with him. He is such a great dad, friend and partner and I feel like the luckiest son (and partner) around! He entrusts me to make decisions and is always there if I need his perspective.

We are a great team but we often see things differently. We think that's OK. Also, our styles are different, but we see the end goal the same; seeing the experience through our guest's eyes and that the guest is our only priority. I wake up every day excited to continue our path to be better, and I am proud and honored that we are doing this journey together!"

———————————— ♦ ————————————

*From Left:* Humberto Gallegos, Patricio Lormendez, Duke, Miguel Hernandez, "Wild" Bill Ranniger, Antelmo "Flacco" Reyes, Rosalio Ulloa Salazar

# Our Talented Chefs

Five of our six Head Chefs were born in Mexico and have worked their way to the top in our kitchens. It's an extremely loyal group; some of these stars have been with us for a decade or longer: Ruston Way Chef Patricio Lormendez (nineteen years), Kent Station Chef Rosalio Ulloa Salazar (seven years), Southcenter Chef Antelmo "Flacco" Reyes (twenty-three years), Alki Chef Humberto Gallegos (eleven years), Lake Union Chef Doug McGrath (fifteen years, not shown) and Green Lake Chef Miguel Hernandez (fourteen years). Also pictured is Executive Chef "Wild" Bill Ranniger, who has been with us for twenty years.

The length of service of our chefs is a tribute to our company and a very good reason why our food has been so good for so many years. Not only have they been with us for a long time, but they also bring happiness to the workplace. Our culture promotes teamwork, mutual respect and a little fun along the way. The result is consistently great-tasting food.

*From Left:* John Moscrip, Kristina Dixon, John Thelen, Marie Dominguez, Duke Moscrip

# Our Trusted Corporate Team

**Kristina Dixon, CFO** (fourteen years). "I love this company, and I am privileged to be a part of a uniquely remarkable team. Duke's passion and integrity in only delivering the very best is an inspiration, and I will do whatever I can to support and help the company grow."

**Marie Dominguez, Administrative Director** (fourteen years). "I love coming to work every day to help support our incredible team whose main focus is giving our guests an amazing dining experience coupled with the most delicious wild and sustainable seafood in the world."

**John Moscrip, Chief Operations Officer** (twenty-five years). "We have the unique opportunity to create special moments with our guests every day. I love that passion and could not imagine doing anything else!"

**John Thelen, Director of Operations** (eighteen years). "The biggest parts of my job are to make sure every guest at Duke's gets great service and also to help our managers succeed in creating an environment where our guests feel welcome and appreciated every time they come in. I drive into work every day with a smile on my face because I love what I do."

**Bill Ranniger, Executive Chef** (twenty years). "I have the greatest job in the world. I get to cook the best ingredients for guests who enjoy the best seafood in the world."

**Duke Moscrip, Chief Executive Officer** (thirty-nine years). "Every great organization needs a team whose members support each other, pull together and keep their eyes on the goals of the company. I am proud to be a part of Duke's exceptional team."

# Our Remarkable People's Performance . . .

## Creates Great Memories For You

We are truly blessed to have so many good people to work with at Duke's. In an era when employers are having difficulty developing loyalty, Duke's is experiencing something quite different. We are honored to have so many great employees, and we have great respect for the job our people do.

───────────── ◆ ─────────────

"Running a restaurant is a difficult task. It requires people to work as a team in order for guests to feel comfortable and cared for. I cannot do it all, our managers and chefs cannot do it all. We require the help of many people. My heartfelt thanks goes out to all of our team members. Without you, we could not provide our guests with a great experience. Thank you. Thank you. Thank you."

───────────── ◆ ─────────────

# Note About My Dad
## By Duke's Daughter, Amy Waeschle

When people find out that my dad is Duke ("Really? That Duke?"), they always assume he cooked for me all the time when I was growing up. I quickly correct them—my dad hardly ever cooked at home. Okay, he did make pretty good omelets and sandwiches, and to this day, his picnics are the best: Kettle chips, Havarti cheese and peanut butter, rotisserie chicken, orange chocolate, and giant cookies. It's what makes him a great restaurateur—his ability to recognize great flavor.

When I was a kid, my dad made the best lunchbox sandwiches. My friends would have their thin little sandwich, with one skinny piece of meat and a hint of mayo and their average, flavorless bread, but I would have my dad's masterpiece. My dad has always had a "go big" attitude toward flavor. "If you're going to make a sandwich," he'd say, "Go big." So he'd bring home big slices of Duke's sourdough bread, pack it full of tuna fish or slices of Tillamook cheddar and real turkey, and add plenty of mayo and a hint of what he called "magic" mustard (always Grey Poupon). As a special treat, sometimes he'd include a cookie from Duke's bakery— they used to have all kinds, including oatmeal raisin, chocolate chip, peanut butter, etc., that were as big as catcher's mitts and earned me looks of envy from my classmates. During my freshman year of high school, I remember suffering through many a pre-lunch math class just dying to crack into my gourmet lunch.

> "If you're going to make a sandwich," he'd say, "Go big."

I love that "Grampa Dude" (as my daughters call him—they couldn't pronounce "Duke" when they were very young) is passing on the tradition of "going big" when making a sandwich. They're not crazy about magic mustard (yet), but they share his passion for flavor, both in food and in life.

My dad is also a little bit crazy. Get him talking about Wild Salmon and you'll see what I mean. He travels to Alaska each year to check on the harvesting of the seafood he buys, something few other restaurant owners ever do. One time, he was visiting a very remote tidal bay, researching razor clams when a brown bear with cubs charged him. Or ask him about the time he agreed to pose with a live 3,200-pound bull inside one of the restaurants. Or when he tried to try out for the Sonics. Ask him about raising money to buy the Mariners to keep them from selling to someone who would move them away from Seattle. You'll find these stories and more like them written in these pages.

He is also very creative and not afraid to try anything. He's taken great risks over the years, and he has been ahead of his time in many trends. The recipes you'll find in this cookbook reflect the hundreds of trials and re-trials on the road to perfection. No flavor nuance has been ignored, and the meals you'll create from this book will make your taste buds buzz with pleasure.

Dig in.

*Grandma, Florence Cox*

*Grampa, John Fitzgerald Cox*

# Growing Up - A Legacy Of Inspiration

Inspiration can come from anywhere. The world is your muse, and it's up to you to discover it. It comes easier for some and is more difficult for others, but each day can be your day to be inspired. The other part of inspiration that isn't mentioned much is motivation. It's the internal engine that constantly drives you to do great things and be proud of those accomplishments. A motor that won't stop running, one that moves you to an endless destination, is something that every inspiration needs to make things happen.

I have always had an engine driving my inspiration, and I give the credit for this to my parents and grandparents. My mom, Ruth, always expected a lot from "her boys," my brother and me. Slacking wasn't in the vocabulary at the Moscrip House. My mom was a taskmaster who ran a tight ship. You did your chores, period, no questions, no negotiations. But she was also very affectionate and loved my brother and me dearly.

My brother Bill and I were always very interested in sports. My dad, the original Duke, was a coach after all, and where he went, we went. But my mom, she had other plans. She didn't want us to "Grow up to be a jockstrap." The funny thing is, she loved sports too and never missed a game we played, but she could always see the bigger picture for us. She understood the valuable leadership, discipline, and

*Mom, Ruth Trana*

*Dad, George Moscrip*

confidence that we were learning in organized sports, but she also had the foresight to push us to do more. When you are young, full of energy and little wisdom, it's easy to think you'll be the next LeBron James or Russell Wilson. My mom always said, "I want you to amount to something; you're not going to spend your life in a gymnasium!" Much of my success in life I attribute to my mom's ambition for me. I can still hear her voice, even now, "Make something of yourself," and I attempt that every day.

My dad was a closet intellectual, hiding out as a coach. He loved kids and loved coaching them. To this day, he is the best coach I've ever had. Kids worshiped him. He was a consummate actor; he could make you laugh and cry, and he could motivate you like no one I've ever seen. His half-time talks were as good as those of Knute Rockne, the famous coach from Notre Dame. In a moment of average performance on the basketball court when I was in seventh grade, he grabbed me by my jersey, lifted me up, looked straight into my eyes, and said to me, "Moscrip, I expect more out of you." In that moment, my heart filled with courage, and I wanted to do nothing more than make my dad proud. He was tough, but in an almost gentle way that made you know he loved you. He instilled a confidence in me and allowed me the freedom to become as good as I could in everything I did throughout my entire life, and my forever running engine and constant inspiration is a testament to his legacy.

# So Why Does Everyone Call Me Duke?

My dad was a pilot in the Navy in World War II and a very flashy dresser as many flyboys were at the time. They had to have the wardrobe to match the fearless attitude and need for speed while flying death-defying missions for their country. He always wore a white scarf, leather cap, and leather jacket, like something straight out of the legend of the Red Baron. They nicknamed him "Duke" because of this. When I was born, I became "Little Duke." The name stuck.

# Bubba aka Big Brother Bill

When I was a little boy, I could not say, "My big brother"; instead, it came out, "My big bubba." Thus the name was born for my big "Bubba" Bill. I worshiped him through my younger years. I was his shadow and only ever wanted to be with "Bubba." He was tolerant mostly and included me in many of his adventures with his buddies, but sometimes he needed his own space and ditched me. That's always so hard to understand at a young age and is a pain only a younger brother can know. It's an emptiness that leaves you feeling a bit abandoned in the moment, and I recall wondering whether Bubba even really liked me.

> "When I was a little boy, I could not say, "My big brother"; instead it came out, "My big bubba."

During this time of being Bubba's shadow, I remember my dad asking a kid whether he wanted to fight me. My dad was always up to some crazy stunt to push us and develop us into "men." The aforementioned kid was much bigger than me and began beating me up. At once, my brother became my shadow, swooped in, and saved me from a terrifying defeat, while the other kid found the business end of my brother's fist. After that day, I never doubted my brother's feelings for me and knew true, unconditional love. To this day, I call him Bubba. Our bond as brothers was unusually strong as kids and remains so today. To say that I love my brother would be an understatement; he has always been there for me, and I will always be there for him.

# Grampa Cox

My grandfather was a character. I would drive him around New England where he would stop and play cards with his cronies. He would play for money, and he seldom ever lost. He could dance like nobody and could drink you under the table. When he was a kid, he broke his arm doing some crazy activity, but he didn't tell his parents for fear he would get whipped. His arm stayed in a permanent slightly bent position as a result, but he never let it bother him. He was as tough as nails. He invented the potato peeler (the patent is in my possession). He made thousands of knives (with the slot for peeling) in his basement on his workbench. He loved to cook, but he also liked going out for dinner and treating his grandkids, my brother and me. He once took us to the Original Toll House before it burned to the ground. I remember stuffing my pockets with free Toll House chocolate chip cookies after dinner.

Duke & Bubba

*Top left picture, from left:* Son-in-law Kurt Waeschle, Daughter Amy Waeschle, Duke, Son John Moscrip, Daughter-in-law Jamie Moscrip

# My Favorite Family

Well, they're my only family, but they are still my favorite! To say that my family means a lot to me would be a gross understatement. They mean everything. Hardly a day goes by that I don't think of every one of them. And the bonus I get is that they are really fun to hang out with. Whether it's dinner out with just the adults or reading books and teasing the grandchildren, the times are precious. I am so lucky to be included in all of their family activities.

Daughter Amy may be the most determined person I know. She takes on a project and holds on like a dog on a bone. She's a wilderness expert, too. You will want her in the foxhole if anything goes bad. She wrote the letter on page 62 when she was young. As you can see, she's got an entrepreneurial spirit as well. Her husband, my son-in-law Kurt, is a great cook, wonderful dad and a guy you want to join you for a beer. He has risen through the ranks to become the head honcho, the fire chief, in the Bremerton Fire Department.

My son John, my partner and my great friend. There is no one more trustworthy in the world and no one more dependable. As a child, he used to count the money in my wallet every night and always knew what time it was. Daughter-in-law Jamie is blessed with a wicked sense of humor and may be the best shopper on the planet. She has made Christmas a dream when I'm looking for just the right thing for just the right person.

# Duke's Grandkids – The Next Generation Of Chefs

If grandchildren are the dessert of life, then mine are the sweetest. Each of my four grandkids is so different yet each possesses a creative spirit and delightful personality that surely is sweeter than all of the desserts put together; my time playing with them leaves me refreshed, like drinking from a fountain of youth. There's Hannah, the horse-lover and the most generous person you've ever met; Hudson, a natural comedian and already a talented athlete who loves everything sports; Elsa, a natural leader, who, like me, rejects rules; and Lauren, full of everything girl, but with a mind for numbers.

*From left:*
Chef Lauren Waeschle, Chef Hudson Moscrip,
Head Sandwich Maker Duke,
Chef Hannah Moscrip, Chef Elsa Waeschle

# How It All Started & The Evolution Of Duke's Brand

From our wild and carefree beginning to Wild Seafood and crazy good food.

# How It All Started —
# A Disastrous Dinner Out
# Changed My Life Forever

In a previous life, I was a relentless stockbroker, but I had a passion for business and food that just wasn't being stimulated with the daily grind of the financial markets. I invested in everything from commodities to precious metals to grape vineyards, and in 1972, with two partners, I bought an interest in Ray's Boathouse.

On opening night, June 30, 1972, my wife at the time and I were having dinner with our friends. We were trying to enjoy our meal, but as I looked around the dining room, all I could see were fidgeting guests, some waving their hands to get their servers' attention, others sighing in frustration or casting awkward glances towards the kitchen.

Bottom line, our guests weren't being taken care of in a proper manner. Granted, opening nights are notoriously challenging—and the restaurant was over-run with people, but I just couldn't handle it. Guests should always receive the best service, no matter what night it is. Right then and there, I rose from the dinner table, put on an apron, got to work, and the rest, as they say, is history. To this day, I am reminded of how I ruined the evening for my dining partners, but it gave me the inspiration and purpose to start this adventure and culture that we have created at Duke's, and that is to take care of people and give them a taste exploration and experience they can't find anywhere else.

Throughout the years, it has been my passion opening and operating Duke's. There have been victories and challenges. I made great decisions and numerous mistakes and almost lost it all several times, but I attempted to learn and grow from every one of my blunders.

Running a restaurant is hard work. I did everything—waited tables, cooked, bartended, ran the kitchen and I loved every minute of it. It is important to know every detail of every job and never be afraid to get your hands dirty. It makes you a better leader and a compassionate boss.

# The Evolution Of Duke's Brand

Back in 1976, Duke's started as a Bar & Grill with ideas inspired by visits to PJ Clarke's in New York, Perry's in San Francisco, The Saloon in Beverly Hills and Jake's in Portland. I measured tables everywhere I went to discover just the exact size that would create an intimate and comfortable feeling for our guests. I photographed the interior of restaurants so I could remember the details I wanted to incorporate. I was even kicked out of the Tadich Grill in San Francisco with my architect for taking photos. I was driven to create something different and fun. I chose blue-checked tablecloths and napkins at the beginning, which have become our trademark look. It seemed to capture the classy but casual atmosphere I was trying to create.

The décor evolved, too, with memorabilia of any person named "Duke" on the wall changing to more and more photos, articles and reviews about Wild Sustainable Seafood sourced mostly from Alaska. I remember when two designers convinced me to paint the walls of the restaurant Chinese red. I never had wanted the color red on the walls, but they assured me that people would feel warm and comfortable. Sure enough, the comments kept coming back, verifying what these talented designers had predicted. That's why you see the red walls in every Duke's.

I sampled food from everywhere, looking for just the right item, the right flavor, the right look. The menu was eclectic, but it soon evolved to seafood after three straight years of winning 1st Place in the Seattle Chowder Cook-Off.

2012 - Present

CHOWDER HOUSE

1988

1976

## Evolution Of Duke's Logo

Our beginning was wild and carefree. I was experimenting as we went. I was attempting to create a fun, casual, classy and unpretentious place to dine and drink. Our plates were decorated with written messages, "Clean Plate Club," "There is no free lunch" and "Life is silly." I paid cash to employees every night, no payroll checks. I issued cigar boxes to our servers and bartenders (no cash registers) and trusted them to turn in the money. We free-poured (no measured shots from a gun) the best liquor you could buy. We served good varietal wine by the glass, which was brand new to the marketplace. It was a happening place. Politicians, celebrities, sports stars, they all showed up.

Unfortunately, much of what we attempted didn't work. We didn't make any money and were financially threatened with closure. But the guests loved the freedom they felt when they came through the door. There were no minimums, no split order charges, and substitutions were not only allowed but encouraged. The guests could run tabs and pay when they felt like it. The bar business took off like a rocket, even though we struggled financially. At some point, I realized we had better start running our business like a business. Some rules were instituted, cash registers were installed, and we avoided the all-too predictable closure of another restaurant. But our core values of taking care of guests survived as well.

Looking back, it was a wonder that we made it. A lot of great people helped along the way, and we just kept plugging along. Pretty soon, we were functioning at a higher level, and we were even starting to make a little money. What a relief!

# Wine By The Glass

Many of you probably don't remember a time before you could order a very nice glass of wine at a restaurant without purchasing the whole bottle. Before this seemingly common "luxury," house wine was generally not the most delicious vintage you could drink. In fact, you were lucky if the "house" wine was on par with a cheap cooking wine, most likely a blend of undesirable leftovers from a vineyard.

In the late summer of 1976, I was sitting in my favorite San Francisco bar with our first Duke's management team. We were preparing to open the first Duke's in Lower Queen Anne and had arranged to get into Henry Africa's early so we could check it out and maybe pick up a few ideas.

On the back bar were 750ml cork-finish bottles with labels "Burgundy," "Rose" and "Chablis." Of course, those aren't varietals, but it was an attempt to have better wine by the glass. Suddenly, it hit me, "Why not serve actual delicious varietals that you would normally only sell by the bottle, but sell them by the glass." Again, I know this seems commonplace, but at the time, it hadn't been done. I proposed it to my team; why not serve glasses of wine of amazing varietals poured from the actual bottles? Why not serve someone a glass of Chardonnay, Sauvignon Blanc, Riesling, Cabernet Sauvignon, Pinot Noir, even Champagne, one glass at a time? Why should restaurants require guests to purchase an entire bottle? We weighed all the risks; what if it didn't work and we had to pour good wine down the drain? The thought was unbearable, but I wanted to bring the best ideas to the table, so to speak, and give people an experience at Duke's that they couldn't get anywhere else. And thus, wine by the glass was born, and we successfully set a trend that would be disappointing and unexpected if it weren't offered at every restaurant today.

Duke and Marketing Director Bettina Carey

# Why Fishing In Alaska Is Just Like Robbing A Bank

When asked why he robbed banks, Willie Sutton, the famous bank robber, said with a smile, "That's where the money is."

A seemingly funny answer to the more ethically directed question at hand, but I draw simplicity from this answer. To get what you want, you go to the most abundant source. So, why do I go to Alaska? That's where the fish are—plentiful, sustainable, natural and wild.

I started sourcing fish from Alaska more than thirty years ago. I honed in on The Copper River long before it became legendary. In fact, the late Jim Callendar, fisherman and former Mayor of Cordova, credited me with putting Copper River Salmon on the map. It was simple—it is an amazing tasting fish so I wanted to serve it at Duke's, and I'm happy that everyone agrees. We also source Salmon from Yakutat with equally stunning results.

The quality of seafood you get at Duke's is unmatched, and I can say that because I personally know exactly how the fish are treated before they arrive at Duke's. I made a commitment to learn how different fishing practices affected the final dishes we served. I wanted only the best for our guests, and the only way to find that was to see it all firsthand.

Alaska is "IT" for wild fish. Over 50 percent of the wild fish consumed in the U.S. comes from Alaska, and it's all wild, not farmed. It is 100 percent sustainable as directed by the Alaska State Constitution, the only state with that directive. My visits have taken me all over the state. Everywhere I've gone, I learned details about what affected the taste of our food. I learned about bleeding fish, icing fish, handling, transporting, how to identify great fish and, most important, how to identify great fishermen and processors.

Duke and Darius Kasprzak,
Rockfisherman in Kodiak, Alaska

# DukeWorthy™ Standards and Specifications for Wild Alaska Salmon and Halibut

After many trips, I developed standards that keep our seafood quality at the highest level, standards I wouldn't have discovered sitting in an office in Seattle. I want only the best for our guests. I have set the bar high for our seafood. Captain Mike Friccero, one of our fishermen, expressed it well when he coined the term, "DukeWorthy." I was out fishing with him on his boat, the Miss Gina, many years ago when a Halibut was being brought in. The fish was of questionable size and did not look vibrant and bright. Mike said, "That's not DukeWorthy; throw it back in the water." From then on, the term stuck and we developed our standards for everything we sourced.

## Troll Fishermen
- Bleed the fish immediately and thoroughly after capture.
- Clean fish within 30 minutes of capture.
- Ice or immerse in refrigerated sea water (RSW) immediately after bleeding and throughout the time before arriving at processing plant. Fish temperature should not exceed 34 degrees F.
- One day old fish only.

## Gill Net Fishermen
- Bleed fish no later than 24 hours after capture.
- Ice fish immediately and throughout the time before arriving at processing plant.

## Processing Plant
- Ice fish from arrival up to the time for fillet, vacuum pack and freezing.
- Fish temperature not to exceed 34 degrees F at any time during processing.
- Head and gut (H & G), then fillet fish immediately. Note: Pin bone fish one day after arrival (difficult to pin bone same day—it tears the fish apart) and then vacuum pack and freeze immediately.

Another option is to send headed and gutted (H & G) fish to Seattle for processing per the above. Minimum 6 large gel packs and ice blanket for each box of Salmon. Air freight to Seattle, same day of processing. Temp fish and accept only fish not to exceed 34 degree F.

## Duke's Standards and Specifications for Wild Alaska Halibut Fisherman
- Bleed the fish immediately after capture and thoroughly.
- Clean fish within one hour.
- Ice or immerse in refrigerated sea water (RSW) immediately after bleeding and throughout time before delivery to processing plant. Maximum temperature is 34 degrees F.
- One to two day old fish only.
- Segregate fish on board by day of catch to insure only one/two day old fish.
- Size 20-40 lbs.

## Processing Plant
- Accept only fish 34 degrees F maximum, clear eyes, firm flesh, skin bright.
- Keep Duke's fish segregated throughout processing.
- Graded #1. No chalky (visual or taste) Halibut accepted.
- Keep fish iced prior to processing, maximum temperature 34 degrees F.
- Fillet, deep-skin, completely bone free, vacuum pack and then freeze at 10 degrees below zero or colder at processing plant.

*Clockwise from top left:* Duke and Halibut in Kodiak, Cordova at Copper River, Thea Thomas and Duke on the Copper River, Duke Cod fishing in Sand Point, Duke temping fish in Copper River

# Why DukeWorthy™ Is More Than Just Great Seafood

Searching for the world's finest seafood and ingredients is my passion. But it's not just about seafood. Whether it's traveling to Chesapeake Bay to visit clammers or blending our custom bourbon at Kentucky's Woodford Reserve, I am in search of natural foods that are chemical-free and sustainably sourced. Buying natural just makes sense to me. The end result is that our guests get really incredible food. Some people think I'm a little over-zealous about our fish, but making sure Duke's provides great tasting food that's also wholesome and doesn't harm the environment is extremely important to me. That's why DukeWorthy™ has become a way of expressing our mission to bring customers the best. It's the reason why we rejected farmed Salmon back when most people thought it was okay (story page 54), why we don't allow foods laced with chemicals like tripolyphosphate, aspartame or sodium nitrite to come into our restaurant. It's why I buy grass-fed beef only from Australia since it's the only country in the world that has had zero outbreaks of E. coli during its entire history. It's why we use dairy products from producers that don't use the artificial growth hormone rBST, and you won't find anything with high fructose corn syrup in our restaurants either. At Duke's, quality matters. We know you are hungry for better food. DukeWorthy™ simply means you get the most wholesome ingredients that are not only better for you, but they just taste better. If it's not DukeWorthy™—we don't serve it.

I have passion for many things, and 100 percent Wild, Sustainable Salmon is one of my highest. I believe in this so much that over the years I have developed close relationships with the fishermen and women from whom we purchase our Salmon. These relationships are incredibly important to me. I

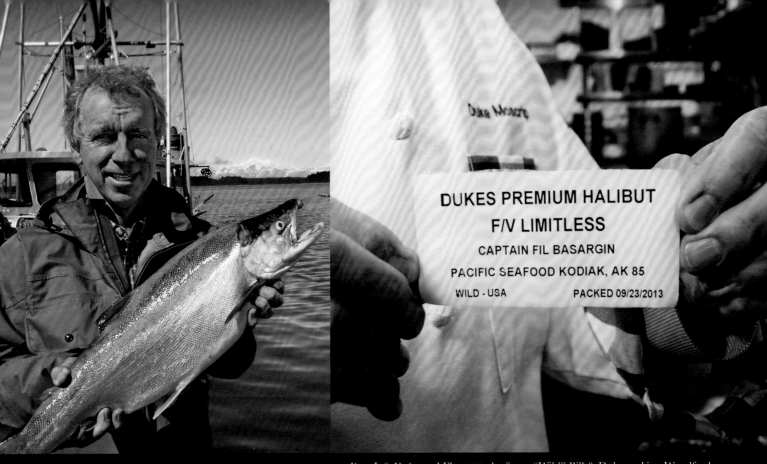

*From Left:* Duke and Flacco at the farm; "Wild" Bill & Duke making Woodford Reserve Bourbon with Chris Morris, Master Distiller; Duke in Yakutat with Salmon; Duke and labels identifying Captain and ship for Halibut.

consider these men and women to be friends and a fundamental part of what makes Duke's so great. Together, we have created a tightly controlled ocean-to-table story that brings in the freshest tasting Salmon commercially available. We are extremely proud to work with these fine, hard-working people and are passionate about how our seafood is harvested, transported and served at Duke's, and it will continue to be the best you will find anywhere. Our guests want to know where their food comes from. They tell us that they choose us because our seafood and operations are Sustainable.

Two years ago, Duke's earned the highest restaurant rating for Sustainable Seafood in the State of Washington by Fish2Fork, an independent rating agency. In fact, no one has a higher rating in the entire world.

Smart Catch is a Sustainable Seafood program with the purpose of increasing sustainable seafood consumption and supporting environmentally Sustainable fishing practices. Duke's is honored to be among the first restaurants in Seattle to be recognized with a 100% Sustainable Seafood rating from Smart Catch.

"Sustainability is very personal to me. I will do everything I can to ensure that my grandchildren and my grandchildren's grandchildren will have wild, natural and Sustainable Seafood to eat and enjoy forever more."

# Farmed Salmon And The Controversial Email

There was this "hot" new trend hitting the restaurant world that promised a streamlined supply chain and consistent "quality" fish. The trend was farmed salmon, and we tried serving it at Duke's for a moment, but I was never crazy about the flavor, and I had to know what the story was.

I started researching farmed salmon processes and found that they are fed pellets containing a dye that makes their flesh red, when, in reality, farmed salmon (if they don't consume these pellets) have flesh that is yellow or grayish color. Wild fish get their vibrant red color from eating Wild Krill and Shrimp. Was this the reason for the inferior flavor as well? We could not get definitive answers. So we decided that the sole solution was to source only 100 percent Wild Salmon and we've been doing it ever since.

Nevertheless, the farmed salmon trend continued and our competitors kept serving it. I felt that I had to say something; I couldn't sit idly by while people I considered friends and family were eating food that I considered to be questionable. So, in May 2003, I penned a controversial email entitled, "You could be getting poisoned if you eat somewhere other than Duke's." In the email, I never said you could get poisoned from farmed salmon, but the inference was clear. I simply shared the facts about the controversial dyes, but I emphasized the bottom line . . . Wild Salmon just tastes better.

Soon after my email, I received an official letter from the attorneys who represent the fish farmers. The message was clear: either I retract my statement about "farmed fish poisoning you," which I never actually stated, or get sued.

I'm a lover, not a fighter, and moreover, I never intended to take on the farmed fish industry. I only meant to inform my friends and family about how I felt. I decided my stance would be simple: farmed fish had its place in feeding the world, it just didn't have any place at Duke's. So in a follow-up email, I apologized and the farmed fish people backed off.

Duke, Mike Looney and Bob Simon
*Top left:* Jimmi Jensen, Duke and Alex Johnson

# I Can't Bear The Thought Of Going Clamming

The photos to the right will tell the story better than I can. Suffice it to say, on one of my illustrious adventures, while in Polly Creek, not too far from Kodiak, Alaska, I got more than I bargained for. Polly Creek is known for being one of the best razor clamming areas in the world. I had to see it for myself, so on one of my trips way up north, I decided to visit this area with Bob Simon of Pacific Seafood.

The area was so secluded that we flew into it on a plane with giant tires that landed on an inclined beach. Imagine a tricked-out float plane with a lift kit and mudding tires as tall as I was. Bob and I hiked about a mile through the mud flats in rubber boots and waders. I remember the suction sound echoing in the still wilderness as, with each step we took, we seemingly sunk deeper into the mud.

As we approached the razor Clam harvesting area, I looked up and saw what I thought was a large dog. I mentioned this to Bob. Bob said, "That doesn't look like a dog, it looks like a huge horse." As we stood still in the mud, I realized it was a huge brown bear with her two cubs. The bear stood on her back legs, turned toward us, took a few steps in our direction and growled. I swiftly turned and started moving as quickly as I could back toward the plane, my feet hurting with each step as I could feel a blister coming on from the constant pull on my boots suctioning in the mud.

The photos on this page tell the story. I looked back at Bob, who had stopped to take a picture. He turned to say something to me, and then realized I was about 50 yards away from him. Bob quickly turned toward me and headed toward the plane.

We didn't look back to see whether the bear and her cubs had started running toward us. I know how fast a bear can run. They are faster than a thoroughbred for forty yards. Yikes! I kept thinking to myself that my job was to outrun Bob. Thankfully, the bears stopped pursuing us. This was definitely an adrenaline rush, but one I don't care to repeat. We made our way safely back to the plane and left unscathed. And, although the bear looks very small in the photo, trust me, it was a big bear. The guy in full retreat is, of course, me attempting to outrun Bob.

GIVE ME ALL YOUR CLAMS

I REMEMBER THE TIRES BEING SOOOOOOOO MUCH BIGGER

BEAR

ME RUNNING FROM BEAR

MY FOOTPRINTS

# Building A Better Community

Giving back to the community has always been a part of Duke's. We have contributed to thousands of charities over the years, and we feel it is our obligation to help out where we can. The following is just some of what we do for the community.

As I recall, the first organization that we helped financially was the Boy's and Girl's Clubs. My dad had coached at the Bellevue Boy's and Girl's Club, and I had grown up there. I always felt I owed a debt of gratitude for all I had received in my many hours at the Club.

Another organization we helped early on was Children's Orthopedic Hospital. My son John had been born premature, so he spent the first six months of his life there. I will always feel the tug at my heart for the great work this organization does.

Early on in our history (mid 1980s), we entered the Seattle Chowder Cook-Off that benefited the Seattle Alzheimer Association. The three first-place ribbons displayed in these pages were the result of our effort to help another worthwhile organization.

We also like to help the Veteran's Hospital. My dad was a veteran who served 35 years in the Navy. He was the original Duke who was a Navy pilot in World War II, and he barely survived an airplane accident when he flew into a mountain in a thunderstorm during training in Phoenix, Arizona. Unfortunately, his co-pilot was not so lucky and did not survive. The Veteran's Hospital got him back to functioning normally. I thank God and bless the doctors at the Veteran's Hospital for helping my father to heal. My heart goes out to each and every veteran. The Veteran's Hospital Mission Statement is "To fulfill President Lincoln's promise to care for him who shall have borne the battle . . . ." It certainly fulfilled that mission for my dad. Now, on International Chowder Day (proclaimed by Mayor Nickels) we donate a portion of our sales for the day to benefit Seattle Veteran's Hospital. Each year, all day on or around Veteran's Day, we serve up thousands of gallons of our three-time champion Award Winning Clam Chowder to guests who come out to support Veterans.

*From Left:* Salmon Sunday at Duke's Green Lake; Fundraiser for Southwest Seattle Historical Society; New Year's Day Polar Bear Swim at Alki Beach; International Chowder Day

When the community of Oso had a tragic mudslide, we held a fund-raising dinner to raise funds for the benefit of the survivors.

At the New Year's Day Polar Bear Swim at Alki Beach in West Seattle, we serve free Chowder to all the participants and spectators, too. It creates a sense of community to all of us involved and brings us all closer together.

I have personally planted trees along the banks of the Snoqualmie River to help rebuild the habitat for Salmon. My son and our Duke's team accompanied me as we did our part to bring back this incredible resource to its glory days when Salmon proliferated in our local rivers. We continue to support Salmon Safe in this endeavor.

We also contribute to Long Live The Kings, another great organization that is working hard to restore Salmon to Northwest waters. Even though Duke's buys its Salmon from Alaska, I am keenly interested in sustainable fisheries everywhere and especially the Northwest where I have grown up and lived. I know we can restore the runs, and we intend to do our part to make it happen.

Recently, we set out to help the Southwest Seattle Historical Society to preserve the history of the area and promote related research and educational efforts. I meant what I said, "We are always happy to help where we are needed. It's wonderful to be a part of the Southwest Seattle Historical Society's efforts to preserve our history."

# Thank you for supporting our efforts!

# Duke Tales . . . Still Mischievous After All These Years

Over the last four decades, I've pulled some crazy stunts. Some were purely marketing fun, but some were serious plots to change the world. Following are a few of my favorites.

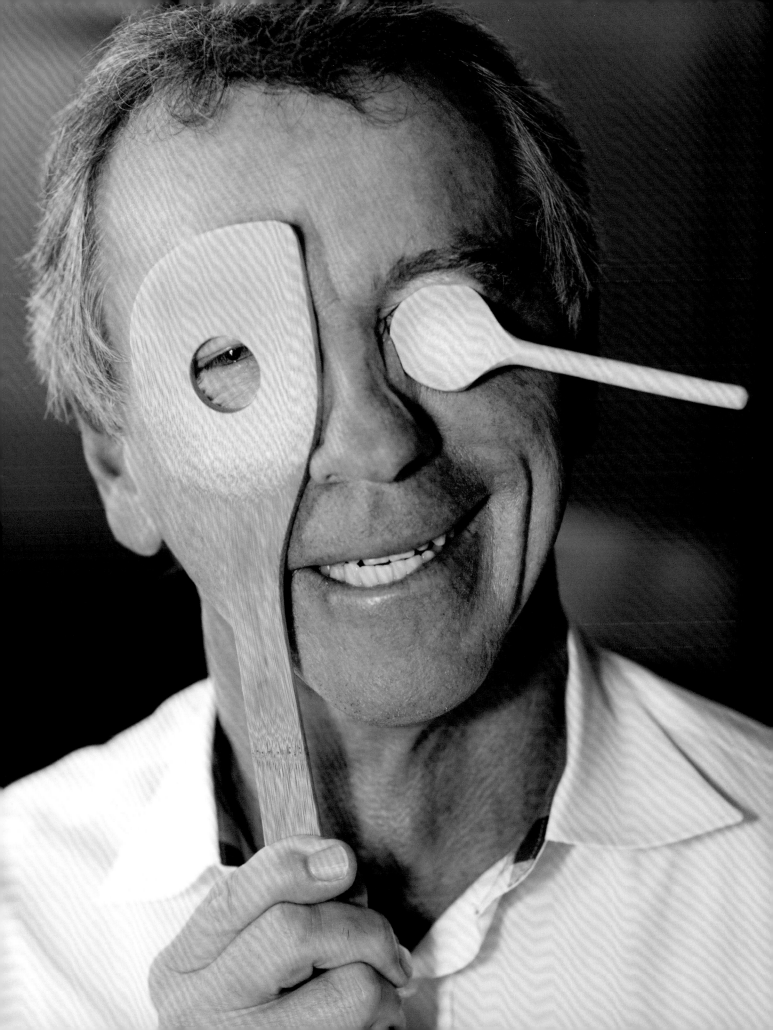

"Sometimes I've been known to use my kid's cuteness for our marketing."

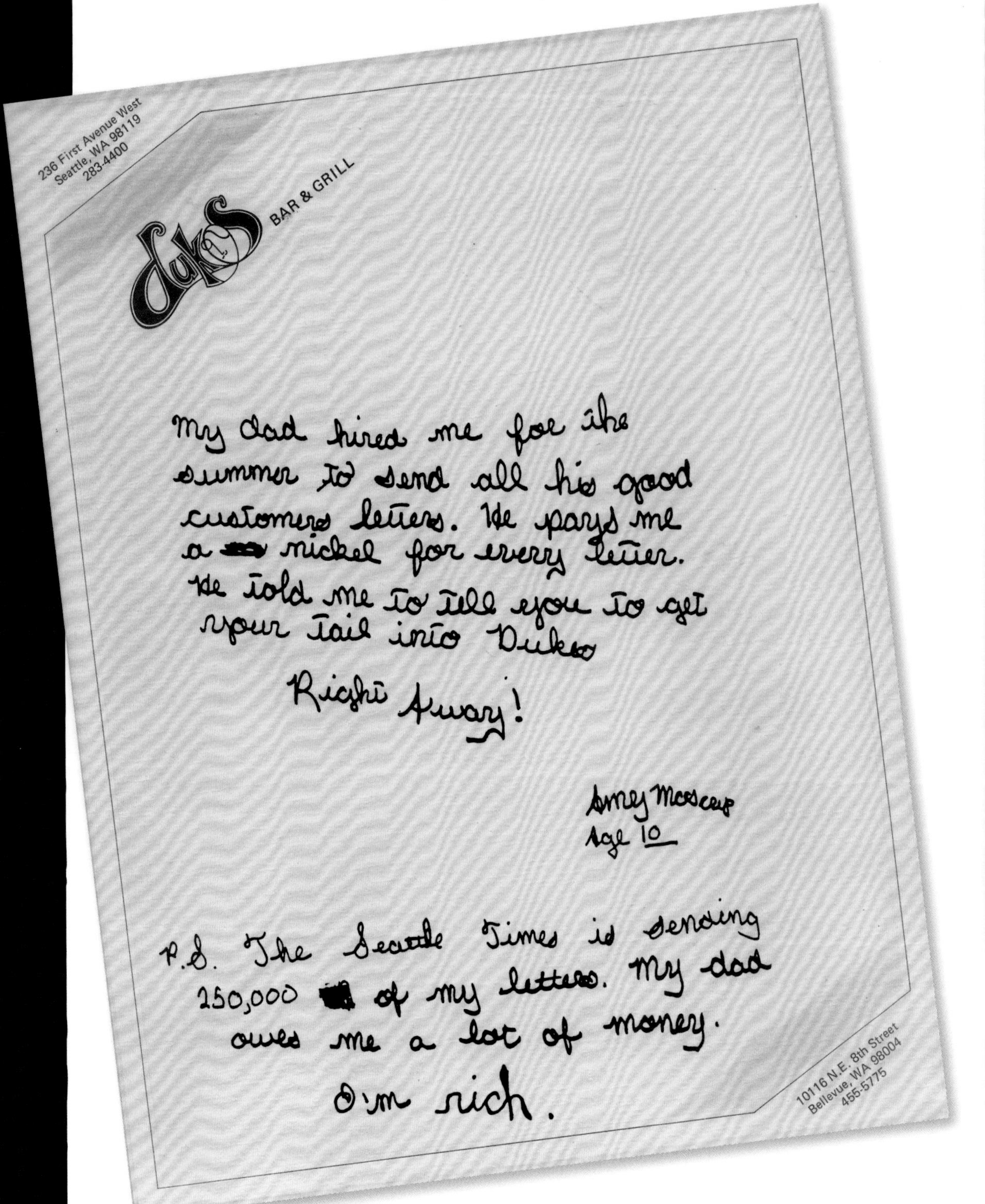

236 First Avenue West
Seattle, WA 98119
283-4400

Duke's BAR & GRILL

My dad hired me for the summer to send all his good customers letters. He pays me a nickel for every letter. He told me to tell you to get your tail into Duke's

Right Away!

Amey Moscup
Age 10

P.S. The Seattle Times is sending 250,000 of my letters. My dad owes me a lot of money.

I'm rich.

10116 N.E. 8th Street
Bellevue, WA 98004
455-5775

"I don't know how to break this to you but you're on the menu."

# Duke And, Yes, That's A Real Bull

Those who know me know I've never been afraid to try something daring to get people excited and interested or to inspire change. Over the years, we've pulled some pretty daring pranks at Duke's, so when advertising guru Dean Tonkin dreamed up the idea of having a live bull sit down for dinner with me at Duke's as a funny way to highlight our steaks, I was nervously intrigued. It was a snarky throwback to my glory days as a stockbroker in a kind of Merrill Lynch type ad, which were very recognizable at the time. I was into the idea and excited to do it until my former wife, Susan, our marketing director at the time, informed me that bulls are the number one killer of farmers.

We could barely fit the bull through the front door of Duke's in Bellevue. We had to use a blue-checked tablecloth as a napkin to tie around his neck, and looking at this nearly two-ton magnificent beast, I was more than a bit terrified. I was supposed to sit there, calm and collected in my tuxedo, nonetheless, seemingly enjoying my dinner! One sudden move or him catching a look at a splash of All Natural Heinz Ketchup on my plate and I would be a dead Duke! Underneath the bull's "napkin" in the photo is a chain that the bull's handler is holding out of the camera's view. Needless to say, it was not the most comfortable situation I've ever been in. The photographers got the shot quickly, and we got that bull out of the restaurant without so much as a scuff on the hardwood floor.

# Leave Poor Herschel Alone

In the late 1980s, a pesky sea lion was eating a lot of Salmon in the canal that connects Puget Sound to Lake Washington near the Ballard Locks. Nicknamed Herschel by the media, he caught the attention of the Washington Fish and Game Department. They tried to remove Herschel, but every attempt failed miserably. They captured and transported him 1,000 miles away, but Herschel returned. They tried to scare him with firecrackers and rubber bullets. But Herschel kept dining on his favorite food, Wild Salmon.

I thought I could help. At least that's what I told the Director of Fish and Game in my letter. I proposed that we would feed Herschel all the Salmon he wanted, and we would pay for it. The director took the bait (pardon the pun), thinking I was serious. (I was not.) I kept a straight face and debated the director on local television. We enjoyed the free publicity while the director looked like an overzealous government official without a sense of humor. Needless to say, Herschel was left alone.

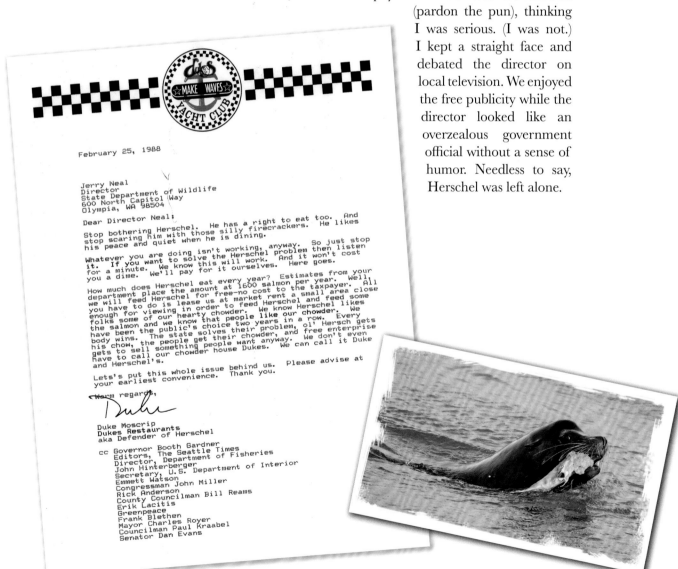

February 25, 1988

Jerry Neal
Director
State Department of Wildlife
600 North Capitol Way
Olympia, WA 98504

Dear Director Neal:

Stop bothering Herschel. He has a right to eat too. And stop scaring him with those silly firecrackers. He likes his peace and quiet when he is dining.

Whatever you are doing isn't working, anyway. So just stop it. If you want to solve the Herschel problem then listen for a minute. We know this will work. And it won't cost you a dime. We'll pay for it ourselves. Here goes.

How much does Herschel eat every year? Estimates from your department place the amount at 1600 salmon per year. Well, we will feed Herschel for free—no cost to the taxpayer. All you have to do is lease us at market rent a small area close enough for viewing in order to feed Herschel and feed some folks some of our hearty chowder. We know Herschel likes the salmon and we know that people like our chowder. We have been the public's choice two years in a row. Every body wins. The state solves their problem, ol' Hersch gets his chow, the people get their chowder, and free enterprise gets to sell something people want anyway. We don't even have to call our chowder house Dukes. We can call it Duke and Herschel's.

Lets's put this whole issue behind us. Please advise at your earliest convenience. Thank you.

Warm regards,

Duke

Duke Moscrip
Dukes Restaurants
aka Defender of Herschel

cc Governor Booth Gardner
Editors, The Seattle Times
Director, Department of Fisheries
John Hinterberger
Secretary, U.S. Department of Interior
Emmett Watson
Congressman John Miller
Rick Anderson
County Councilman Bill Reams
Erik Lacitis
Greenpeace
Frank Blethen
Mayor Charles Royer
Councilman Paul Kraabel
Senator Dan Evans

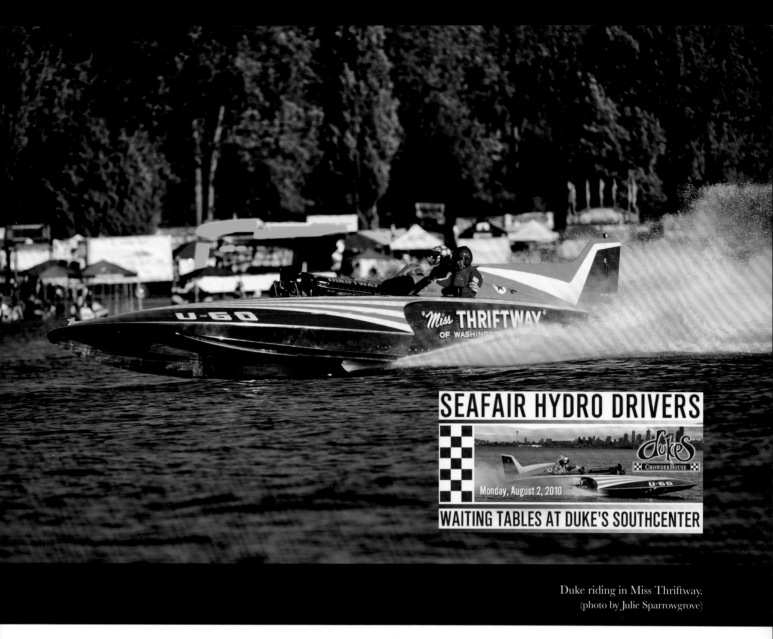

Duke riding in Miss Thriftway.
(photo by Julie Sparrowgrove)

# Some Say I Saved Seafair

When the drivers of the hydroplanes balked at taking a pay cut for the Seafair Race in 2010, I decided to step up. When I was in fifth grade, my brother and all our buddies used to carve hydroplanes out of wood and tie them to the back of our bicycles. We towed them all over the neighborhood, racing each other. We were hooked on hydros then and love them to this day.

I didn't want anything to happen to the hydroplane race, so I called my friend, Chip Hanauer, at the time the winningest hydro driver of all time. I wanted his help at a press conference. He introduced me and said that I had a plan. I announced that I would fund the amount of money needed to make the drivers financially whole and keep them happy. Without the money, the drivers threatened not to race and Seafair would have been threatened with its very existence. No drivers, no race. No race, no Blue Angels. It was a dicey situation. Many think I saved Seafair. Let's just say that without my help, Seafair was in big doubt.

# The Time I Tried To Try Out For The Sonics

In the fall of 1977, it was announced that the Seattle SuperSonics would relocate from The Seattle Center Coliseum to the Kingdome. Naturally, I wasn't happy about this change of venue because it took the SuperSonics out of our neighborhood. In response, I ran a full page ad in the Sonics program, using the photo on this page of me in my friend Jack Sikma's uniform. The ad said, "I'm depressed. First the Sonics moved to the Kingdome and then Lenny (coach at the time) cancelled my tryout. Come cheer me up tonight at Duke's." It worked; the fans returned. I'm still waiting for my try out.

Back before the Sonics won a world championship in 1979, there was one place you had to be for a pre-game warm up or post-game meltdown: Duke's Restaurant on Queen Anne.

It's nice to know that some things haven't changed.

Duke's Queen Anne Chowder House is still the unofficial hangout for thirsty and hungry Sonics loyals. And a pretty darn good place to catch all the action.

Of course there are now four Duke's Chowder House Restaurants, each dedicated to serving good food in a fun atmosphere. Just because the Queen Anne Duke's is right by KeyArena doesn't mean you have to go there on a Sonics game night. We celebrate the Sonics at all our Duke's locations.

We can't promise that the Duke of Chowder, Duke Moscrip, will always be there. You can see from the photo that he's a pretty busy guy on game nights.

**dukes**
**CHOWDERHOUSE**
Eat. Drink. Relax.

# The Unofficial Sonics Pre-Game Show

# My Letter To Pete Carroll

A few days after the Seahawks lost the "Big Game" to New England in 2015, I dreamed up an idea. Losing the "Big Game" the way they did made a lot of fans angry with the coaches. They had been ready to score what looked like an easy touchdown in the final minutes of the game, but they'd thrown a pass instead. The pass was intercepted and it cost them the championship. I wanted to do something to help us all get past the devastating loss. It seemed to me that Pete Carroll and the Seahawks coaches would surely appreciate some help. The players have the 12th Man, but Pete and the coaches didn't have a Man. That's why I introduced the 13th Man. I thought then, and I still believe now, that the 13th Man is just what the coaches needed.

Duke's CHOWDER HOUSE

INTRODUCES

THE

13TH MAN

Brought to you by Duke's CHOWDER HOUSE

Fully Inflated

ALKI
206-937-6100

GREEN LAKE
206-522-4908

KENT STATION
253-850-6333

LAKE UNION
206-382-9963

SOUTHCENTER
206-243-5200

TACOMA
253-752-5444

**Open Letter to Pete Carroll and all Seahawks Coaches**

Dear Pete,

I know you are just as disappointed in Sunday's result as any fan and probably even more so. It was a devastating loss. There is frustration everywhere and a fair amount of anger floating around. But I have an idea that can turn things around. Here it is. The players have the 12th Man to help them out but you don't have a Man. Let me introduce the 13th Man for you and the Coaches. I know the number 13 is usually unlucky but, in this case, it is just the opposite. With the enormous amount of bad luck in the 'Big Game', we need a strong antidote and No. 13 will do the job. I once intercepted a pass in the end zone and ran for a 103 yard touchdown when I was in Pee Wee football. I was wearing, you guessed it, No. 13. It worked for me and it will work for you. The 13th Man will provide wonderful ideas for you and all the coaches, trick plays, a modern day Statue of Liberty play, sneaky stuff to make your opponents just as frustrated as all of us are right now. Consider the 13th Man your lucky charm. You know what they say, you can never have too much good luck. I hope you will see this as a positive thing for your coaches and team. We need to be positive from here on out. Yes, we lost the 'Big Game' but we just have to move on and the 13th Man will help us do that. What do you say, Pete?

Duke Moscrip

P.S. To help ease everyone's distress, the 13th Man has made arrangements to buy all Seahawk fans a FREE small bowl of chowder with purchase of any food item! All they have to do is bring a copy of this letter or show it on their phone at any one of our six locations.

www.DukesChowderHouse.com

# Let's Buy Out George

This was the title of an advertisement I placed in The Seattle Times and The Seattle Post-Intelligencer back in the late 1980s when George Argyros, then owner of the Seattle Mariners, wanted to sell the team and purchase the San Diego Padres. I couldn't bear the thought of the Mariners leaving town, so I had to do something. George had a long history in Seattle of "baseball on the cheap" since buying the team in 1981. He was notorious for not wanting to pay the kinds of salaries needed to obtain and retain good talent. The Mariners at that time had the lowest payroll of any franchise in all of Major League Baseball. When he signed a letter of intent with San Diego, the Seattle fans were outraged, and old George didn't attend a single home game after opening night. I don't think he could handle all the boos that echoed throughout the Kingdome since they were all for him.

In response to the ad, many people sent me money. I was on the front page of the Times. I advocated for the public and touted that we could own the team just like the Green Bay Packers, who are publically owned by their fans. I arranged a private meeting in Orange County at George's office. He told me to keep our negotiations totally confidential and private. George was intrigued with my idea, but he didn't want a protracted period to raise the money. He wanted to sell, and he wanted the cash now. At the secret meeting, he told me I would have to raise the money privately and quietly or he would cut off negotiations.

I worked behind the scenes and had commitments for nearly $10 million before Jeff Smulyan came along and offered $75 million while I was out beating the bushes for investors. Our dream of public ownership was shattered, but the effort was long remembered by Seattle baseball fans. I was the guy who tried to save the Mariners.

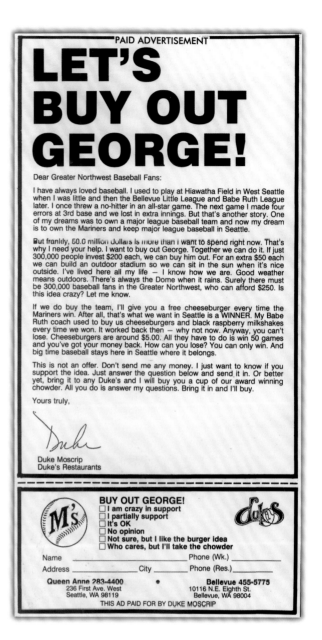

# The Time I Tried To Be
# The Seahawks Quarterback

July 31, 1999

Mike Holmgren
Seattle Seahawks
11220 N E 53rd Street
Kirkland, WA 98033

Dear Coach Holmgren:

I couldn't help notice your photo in the newspaper and the article which talks about you looking for "bangers." I'm no banger but I can do something better. I can throw the bomb. My favorite play when I was a Quarterback in PeeWee Football and Bellevue Junior High was to throw the bomb on the first play of the game. I'd fade back and throw it as far as I could. Someone on our team would always catch it for a touchdown. What a play that was. And I once scored a touchdown on a 103 yard pass interception. I played both sides of the ball then but that's another story.

Right now my dream is to play QB for the Seahawks. You don't have to bring me in as a starter right away. I'm willing to earn my position. I just want a chance to compete and show you I can play. Here's the deal I'll make with you. When I was a PeeWee, our coach (my dad) would buy us milk shakes (any flavor we wanted) and cheeseburgers every time we won. I'll go one better. I'll buy milk shakes, cheeseburgers AND our Award Winning Clam Chowder at any of our four Duke's Chowder Houses for everyone on the team every time we win. All you have to do is put me on the team. What have you got to lose? You get a great QB, the team wins and all the players eat like Kings at Duke's.

Call me any time at 206 283 4452. I'll be warming up my arm.

Your QB of the future,

Duke Moscrip

P.S. Here's a gift certificate for you and your family. I don't want you making any decisions on an empty stomach.

# The Sidewalk Caper

It was insanely hot in the summer of 1984. Even though we had air conditioning, people seemed to find their way to waterfront restaurants and outside decks. (This situation contributed greatly to our later pursuit of just that—waterfront locations with outside decks.) I learned that Seattle people just love being outside whenever they can. I needed a trick to get guests to come back. So I painted the sidewalk in the Duke's checked blue and white to match our tablecloths.

It didn't take long for the City of Seattle to notice and demand that I sandblast the paint off the sidewalk. Meanwhile, guests were trickling in, curious about the sidewalk. I have to admit it gave the old gray, boring sidewalk a nice lift. I asked a frequent patron, the mayor at the time, Charlie Royer, for help. He told me he really liked the paint job and would see what he could do. Meanwhile, the press discovered what I had done and the city's crusade to sandblast it. Petitions with "SOS"—"Save our Sidewalk" were circulated and signed by hundreds of guests. The city was relentless. Charlie was able to put them off for a period while we contemplated our next move.

The press loved it and wrote about the "Big City Government vs. the small business owner just having a little fun in the middle of a heat wave." Guests flooded in and the conflict was nothing but fun for everyone . . . save for the city officials. Later that year, The Seattle Times placed the story in their "Top Ten" stories of the year. Later, we were forced to remove the paint, which prompted a "blast off" party, and the fun ensued again.

# Live Long Enough To Live Forever

The real truth about food.

DISCLAIMER: I am not a real doctor, even though I occasionally like to dress up like one. Please consult a real doctor for all health questions or issues.

On the other hand, I do have opinions about food, nutrition, and health. I am a research fanatic and read everything I can get my hands on about food, health, and longevity. I want food not only to taste good, but also to be nutritious and healthful. We strive for this in our restaurants.

# Fountain Of Youth

I went to college planning to become a doctor. Although I was led in a different direction with my passion for business and food, I have always held an interest in health, nutrition and cures for diseases. After being in the restaurant business for a few years, I continued my learning in the field of health and science and began applying what I was learning from scientific studies to my business. This allowed two of my passions (great flavor and health) to join together to serve our guests.

This interest has led me to eliminate from our restaurants foods like trans fats, farmed salmon, aspartame, grain-fed beef, high fructose corn syrup, soy lecithin and other ingredients that many believe to be questionable as food items or because of adverse environmental effects—and often years before doing so was a common trend. The minute I discover something is controversially unhealthy, we take it off the menu and replace it with what we believe to be a more wholesome alternative. I by no means have all the answers, but I am passionate about good, wholesome food, and you have my word that everything on our menu is what we believe to be the best that nature has to offer.

I have always believed in the power of food. In its purest form, food is the abundance of healthy living and can always be delicious. Just because it's good for you doesn't mean it can't taste amazing, too. I believe that good, wholesome food is the most important driver in the quest to live forever.

Wholesome doesn't necessarily mean some kind of strange health food; it's just food without additives, natural, the way it exists in, well, nature. You can combine so many wholesome ingredients to create flavors you never thought possible and feel good about what you're putting in your body as well. Now, I'm not going to sit here and tell you everything on our menu is perfect for every person, but it is wholesome from the source and is only made with the best ingredients. After all, we need food for the body, mind and soul. That's where treats like chocolate cake and ice cream come in.

# The Quest For Perpetuity

I believe it is possible to live forever—well, almost forever. When I share this idea with friends, I do get some pretty strange looks. I can see their facial reactions that say, "Are you crazy?" But books like *Fantastic Voyage: Live Long Enough to Live Forever—The Secret Behind Radical Life Extension* by Ray Kurzweil, support my "crazy" theory.

Here's my theory of Perpetuity. My goal is to do everything in my power to stay healthy and vibrant until I am eighty-nine. I believe that if you eat well and take care of yourself, you can be the best version of yourself health-wise into your late eighties. As nature takes its toll on our aging bodies, new science developments help offset those natural tendencies of bones breaking down, muscles deteriorating, etc. But if you stay active and eat well, you can slow this process down on your own. If you slow it down just enough, the advances in medical science will deliver life-extending miracles.

When I reach the age of eighty-nine, I believe biotechnologies will deliver a mega-dose of anti-aging discoveries that will take me, fully healthy and vibrant, to the age of 129. As medical science continues to advance, I will comfortably be taken to the age of 199. At age 199, medical science will deliver the final coup de grâce that will take me to Perpetuity. I want you to join me. The key to my theory is to stay healthy for as long as you can while medical science brings cure after cure after cure. Eating at Duke's won't guarantee you a long life, but it will surely help to keep you in the game.

But don't just take my word for it; check out Ray Kurzweil's aforementioned book and read the words in the next few pages of my friend and kindred spirit, Dr. Brad Weeks, M.D., N.D., who believes that food is medicine and who has given Duke's his stamp of approval.

199

129

89

AGE

# The Doctor Is In -
# Bradford S. Weeks, M.D., N.D.

I am a medical doctor who uses food as medicine, and for decades, I have taught my patients that a healthy diet can make many, if not most, drugs redundant and obsolete. There are no miracle drugs, nor are there miracle foods; the human body itself is the miracle worker. Our responsibility is to take care of our miraculous body, feed and hydrate it well and use it appropriately.

My patients know I disagree with the term "junk food." In my opinion, there is no junk food. There is food, and there is junk, and even though the junk might be full of artificial flavors and artificial sweeteners and artificial colorings—making it edible and perhaps even delicious—it is not food. Food, by definition, nourishes. Junk does not.

Sadly, some restaurants today offer junk that is labeled as food, but it is laced with chemicals, artificially colored or genetically altered. In order to obtain good quality food, customers are forced to ask specifically for it. "Is that salmon wild, or is it farm-raised?" or "What type of oil are you frying with?" Sometimes, people wanting to eat food and not junk seem to talk in code to the waiter. It might sound like this: "I need my meal to have no SL, HFCS, TFA, MSG or rBST. OK?"

At Duke's, they understand this code. "No problem," your waiter would say. Duke's is one of the rare restaurants with no junk. The magnificent book you hold in your hands reflects the passion and commitment of a master restaurateur and his brilliant chef who create top-quality, delicious meals that are natural, sustainable and, most important, as good as medicine.

Note from *Duke*:

People with Celiac Disease: Each of the recipes in this book designated gluten-free (gf) have ingredients so that people who have a desire to avoid gluten in food products can do so. Your kitchen may not be gluten-free and we cannot guarantee that ingredients of recipes that are gluten-free have not come in contact with gluten products during their preparation in your kitchen.

# Dr. Weeks' Comments On Specific Ingredients

## Trans Fats

Trans Fatty Acids (TFA), typically found in baked goods and deep-fried foods, are synthetic and created by destroying healthy oils in order to preserve foods. The problem is that Trans Fatty Acids increase the risk of many illnesses, including cancer and heart disease, because they interfere with normal healthy metabolism. It may seem contrary, but my advice is to eat only food that will rot or turn rancid. That is living, real food. Junk never rots, and that should tell you something! Duke's has no Trans Fats on its menu.

## Gluten-Free Options

Gluten, a protein in wheat, can cause many chronic inflammatory and degenerative illnesses by interfering with normal digestion. For many people, avoiding gluten may eliminate more than 250 symptoms, not just digestive problems but many neurological and auto-immune diseases as well. It is very difficult to eliminate gluten in a restaurant, yet Duke's is committed to offering many gluten-free choices.

## High Fructose Corn Syrup

High Fructose Corn Syrup (HFCS) is a synthetic substance, which, even in moderation, can cause heart disease, obesity, cancer, dementia, liver failure, eye problems, tooth decay and certain endocrine diseases. HFCS is rapidly absorbed and wreaks havoc with insulin secretion, stimulating harsh cravings. Duke's has no High Fructose Corn Syrup on their menu.

## Soy Lecithin

Soy lecithin (SL), synthetically derived almost universally from non-organic, genetically-modified crops (GMO), is an inhibitor of healthy enzymes and compromises the human body's ability to digest food and be nourished. Avoiding soy lecithin can help avoid many diseases linked to poor digestion, including auto-immune illnesses, pre-menstrual pain, fertility problems and inflammatory conditions such as allergies and endometriosis. Duke's has no soy lecithin on their menu. Fermented soy (such as in soy sauce) has none of the properties of soy lecithin.

## Lots of Natural Fish Oil

Eating wild fish such as Salmon is excellent for our health because of its rich supply of Omega-3 fatty acids, which decrease triglycerides and have been linked to benefits such as lowering inflammation and increasing mental ability. The best way to get these benefits is simply to eat fish. Duke's has plenty of great choices.

## No Preservatives

Sodium nitrate, a preservative commonly added to cured meats such as bacon and grain-fed beef, is linked to cancer. It converts to the carcinogen nitrosamine, damages blood vessels and is implicated in heart disease and diabetes. Duke's serves only grass-fed beef, which has no nitrates, and meat with no sodium nitrite.

## No Growth Hormones

The growth hormone known as BGH/BST or Recombinant bovine somatotropin (rbST), sold under the name Posilac, has been banned since 2000 in Canada, Australia, New Zealand, Japan, Israel, the European Union and Argentina due to cancer risk in humans and the negative health effects on cows. Duke's butter, milk, cream and buttermilk are supplied by local producer Darigold and contain zero growth hormones.

## Coffee

Coffee has many anti-oxidant benefits, but most coffee is farmed using pesticides. These pesticides intoxicate our lipophilic cell membranes. Duke's serves only organic coffee from Caffe Ladro (owned by Duke's good friend Jack Kelly), which contains no pesticides.

## All Natural Stevia as an Alternative to Artificial Sweeteners

Used in moderation, sugar is safer than artificial sweeteners. Artificial sweeteners contain an excitotoxin, which is a chemical that intoxicates and stresses the brain. Artificial sweeteners can be addictive and neuro-toxic, and they are implicated in many illnesses, including headaches, memory loss, seizures, vision loss, coma, cancer, fibromyalgia, MS, lupus, ADD, diabetes, Alzheimer's, chronic fatigue and depression. Duke's offers Stevia, a naturally sourced sweetener extracted from the Stevia Rebaudiana plant. I know for a fact that Duke uses it in his tea.

## Sea Salt

Conventional salt contains anti-caking additives like yellow prussate of soda, sodium aluminosilicate and cynanide in the form of Sodium ferrocyanide, Potassium ferrocyanide, Calcium ferrocyanide and dextrose. Yes, even commercial salt has sugar added! Sea salt is simply evaporated seawater. Duke's uses only sea salt in its kitchen.

## Organic Herbs

Organic herbs are far safer and more beneficial than non-organic herbs because the seeds and oils of a plant are where pesticides, herbicides and heavy metals are stored. Duke's serves fresh organic herbs.

## Organically Fed and Cage-Free Chickens and Eggs

If there is a hell on earth, it is what caged chickens experience. Hens raised in factory settings are crammed together so tightly that they require prophylactic antibiotics. They are also denied natural behaviors like pruning, perching, nesting and dust bathing. The chickens and eggs served at Duke's are cage-free.

## Grass-Fed Beef

Grass-fed organic meat is leaner, and its fats are more heart-healthy than corn-fed beef. Meat from feedlot animals fattened on corn typically has 15 to 50 percent less omega-3s compared to beef raised on natural grass. Also, grass-fed cows create a healthier world for us because they have less antibiotic resistance, cause less environmental degradation, heart disease, E. coli infection and water pollution.

## No MSG

Mono sodium glutamate, or "MSG," is an artificial compound used for flavoring food that is linked to negative health effects such as headache, dizziness, nausea and weakness as well as flushing and sweating and other neurological symptoms like numbness and tingling or burning in the face and neck. Cardiac symptoms may include fast and irregular heartbeat and chest pain. Duke's uses no MSG in any recipe.

gf = gluten-free recipes

# Secret Recipes Revealed

At Duke's, seafood is our passion. These are the recipes that built Duke's.

# Appeteasers & Shared Plates

Everyone loves a tease.

# TOPLESS WILD ALASKA SALMON SLIDERS

We're always a little nervous when a party of two orders this—fights have broken out over the third slider. Don't worry; we keep a stocked first-aid kit (and extra sliders) at the ready. Just to be safe, you may want to double the recipe at home.

Serves two as an appeteaser

## Ingredients

Three 1¼ oz Wild Alaska Salmon Fillets

½ tsp Duke's Ready Anytime Seasoning (pg 323)

½ tsp Let's Be Clarified Butter (pg 148)

1 slice Essential Baking Company Rosemary Bread cut in 3 pieces

1 Tbsp Basil Almond Pretty Pesto (pg 320)

3 half slices tomato

## Directions

- Fillet Salmon using the deep-skin method, which is to remove the gray matter along with the skin and pluck the pin bones with needle-nose pliers or boning tweezers. If you are buying from your local fishmonger, ask to have the fillet deep-skinned as well.

- Season Salmon pieces with Ready Anytime Seasoning and grill them on medium-high in ¼ tsp of Let's Be Clarified Butter. They will cook very quickly, 3-4 minutes.

- Cut bread into three portions and grill in remaining Let's Be Clarified Butter. Then smear each slice with ½ tsp Basil Almond Pretty Pesto.

- Add tomato and hot Salmon and then top with remaining Basil Almond Pretty Pesto.

# WILD ALASKA SALMON CAESAR SHOOTS gf

If this recipe were an infomercial, here's what it would sound like: Salads are amazing—don't get me wrong—but first you need a bowl, utensils, a napkin, a chair, a table . . . the list goes on. Now, imagine I told you that you could have all the comforts of a salad without any of the accessories . . . an Alaska Salmon Caesar Salad you can eat with your hands! This is a Caesar salad combined with Salmon all wrapped up for an easy-to-eat finger food. Leave the utensils in the drawer and let your fingers get grabbin'!

Serves two as an appeteaser

## Ingredients

5 pieces Wild Alaska Salmon, about 1¼ oz each

1 tsp Blackening Spice Of Life (pg 323)

1 Tbsp Let's Be Clarified Butter (pg 148)

5 romaine lettuce shoots

2 Tbsp All Hail Caesar Salad Dressing (pg 136)

1½ tsp Parmesan cheese and 1½ tsp Asiago cheese, grated and combined

2 Tbsp fresh tomatoes, diced

## Directions

• Fillet Salmon using the deep-skin method, which is to remove the gray matter along with the skin and pluck the pin bones with needle-nose pliers or boning tweezers. If you are buying from your local fishmonger, ask to have the fillet deep-skinned as well.

• Dredge Salmon in Blackening Spice Of Life.

• On a flat griddle or in a sauté pan, heat Let's Be Clarified Butter and sauté Salmon until caramelized.

• Nestle one grilled Salmon portion inside each romaine shoot. Drizzle with dressing and sprinkle with cheese. Top with tomatoes.

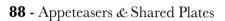

# WILD ALASKA SCALLOP PROVIDER'S SLIDERS

Aboard the ship *M/V Provider*, owned by my friend Jim Stone and his partners in Alaska, the crew freezes the Scallops they harvest immediately, which preserves their sweet, fresh taste. On a fishing trip with the crew, I ate a raw Scallop just moments after it came out of the ocean. The fresh, sweet and salty taste made me marvel at how surprisingly delicious they were. (Don't worry; we cook yours.) They are firm but then melt in your mouth. The combination of fresh ingredients in these sliders will give you an out-of-body food experience.

Note: A slider is usually a small sandwich served in a bun or open-faced. Sometimes they are called "mouth amusements," from the French term, amuse bouche. In reality, a slider is anything with great flavor that slides down the gullet with grace and dignity.

Serves one as an appeteaser

## Ingredients

1 Alaska Weathervane Scallop (size 10 to 20 Scallops per lb)

1 slice (crostini size) from a loaf of Essential Baking Company Sourdough Bread

pinch Duke's Ready Anytime Seasoning (pg 323)

1 tsp extra virgin olive oil

⅛ avocado, sliced thin and fanned

1 tsp Sinful Citrus Vinaigrette (pg 138)

1 tsp Dukecumber Pico de Gallo (pg 275)

## Directions

- Prepare crostini first. Cut ¼ inch-thick slice of sourdough bread. Cut in half and grill in ½ tsp of olive oil on both sides until crispy.

- Season Scallop with Duke's Ready Anytime Seasoning.

- On a flat griddle or sauté pan, heat ½ tsp olive oil. (Oil needs to be hot for the Scallop to obtain that golden brown color.)

- Sear Scallop on both sides until caramelized (about 1½ minutes per side).

- Place fanned avocado on grilled bread and drizzle with Sinful Citrus Vinaigrette. Add Dukecumber Pico de Gallo and top with Scallop.

# PRAWNS DEL CABO WABO gf

We have eleven incredibly talented Hispanic Head Chefs and Sous Chefs at Duke's. They understand flavor in a way a gringo like me can only admire. Traditional Mexican food is healthy and bursting with fresh flavors. The blend of fresh organic herbs and citrus vinaigrette in the recipe below is a tribute to these enormous flavors.

Serves two as an appeteaser

## Ingredients

6 Wild Mexican Prawns (size 21-25 per lb)

1 tsp extra virgin olive oil

pinch fresh garlic, diced small

pinch fresh organic basil, julienne-sliced

pinch Duke's Superb Herb Blend (pg 322)

1 Tbsp fresh organic cilantro, diced small

2 Tbsp Sinful Citrus Vinaigrette (pg 138)

Avocado Tower Salad (see below)

## Directions

• Peel, devein, rinse and dry Prawns.

• Marinate with extra virgin olive oil, garlic, basil and Duke's Superb Herb Blend for at least an hour.

• Sear Prawns on a hot flat griddle or sauté pan and arrange on plate.


# AVOCADO TOWER SALAD gf

## Ingredients

½ fresh avocado, diced medium

2 Tbsp Dukecumber Pico de Gallo (pg 275)

juice from half of a lime

1 tsp extra virgin olive oil

pinch Duke's Ready Anytime Seasoning (pg 323)

½ tsp Duke's Superb Herb Blend (pg 322)

## Directions

• Gently combine ingredients, (do not over-mix or avocado will turn to mush.) Place in a stainless steel tower mold (approximately 2-inch by 2-inch by 2-inch cube); then release on plate.

# KILLER PRAWNS

No, these are not some new form of scary sea monster you have to look out for on your next snorkeling trip. These Prawns are just so good our servers call them "killer" good.

Serves two as an appeteaser

## Ingredients

5 Wild Mexican Prawns (size 21 to 25 per lb), peeled and deveined

1 Tbsp extra virgin olive oil

pinch crushed red pepper flakes

pinch Duke's Superb Herb Blend (pg 322)

pinch fresh organic basil leaves, stems removed, diced small

1 Tbsp fresh garlic, diced small

1 Tbsp Roasted Garlic Cloves (pg 328)

¼ cup red pepper, roasted and julienne-sliced

pinch Duke's Ready Anytime Seasoning (pg 323)

pinch fresh organic parsley, stems removed, diced small

¼ cup white wine

6 Tbsp Garlic Lover's Butter (pg 148)

6-inch long sourdough baguette (for dipping)

## Directions

• Sauté Prawns in olive oil until just seared on both sides.

• Add crushed red peppers, Superb Herb Blend, basil, fresh roasted garlic, red pepper, Ready Anytime Seasoning and parsley. Cook until the Prawns are ¾ done (about 3 minutes).

• Deglaze the pan with white wine (Deglazing, Demystified, pg 326).

• Add 4 Tbsp Garlic Lover's Butter, and remove from heat. Swirl to incorporate.

• Cut baguette into ⅛-inch slices. Spread each with Garlic Lover's Butter, and bake at 400 degrees until crisp, approximately 4 minutes.

**DukeWorthy Provider**

## Consistently The Best Tasting Prawns In The World

Meridian – Your Prime Seafood Source has provided Wild Mexican Shrimp to Duke's for several years. Ana Rodriguez of Meridian said, "We really admire Duke's diligence and pursuit of the best Shrimp in the world."

I love the firmness of these Shrimp, the special Shrimp flavor that tastes like it just came out of the ocean. Located near Mazatlan, this fishery continually produces the best of the best.

**YOUR PRIME Meridian SEAFOOD SOURCE**

# COCO LOCO PRAWNS

I have tasted Prawns from all over the world, and the Wild Mexican Prawns caught off the west coast of Mexico are the best. Combined with coconut, they are simply spectacular! Serve them at a party and they'll disappear faster than coconuts off a palm tree in a windstorm.

Serves two as an appeteaser

## Ingredients

5 Wild Mexican Prawns (size 21-25 per lb), peeled and deveined

1 "In Your Cups" Parmesan cup (pg 330)

1 cup coconut milk

½ cup tempura flour (we use Krusteaz)

½ cup panko breadcrumbs (available at most grocery stores)

½ cup shredded sweetened coconut

½ cup Thai One On Sweet Chili Sauce (pg 279)

¼ cup Duke's Coltrane Coleslaw (pg 280)

GMO-free canola oil for frying

 Tip from Chef "Wild" Bill:

These Prawns are not only delicious; they are also sustainable. When purchasing your Prawns, make sure your provider uses TEDs (Turtle Excluder Devices) so the turtles will stay safe.

## Directions

• Peel and devein Prawns, leaving tails on, and place in refrigerator.

• Make the batter by whisking together coconut milk and tempura flour.

• Combine panko with shredded coconut and set aside.

• Coat Prawns in coconut milk batter by holding the tails and dunking several times, allowing excess batter to drip off between dunks.

• Press Prawns into panko mixture. Refrigerate.

• Heat oil in Dutch oven or thick-sided soup pot. Heat oil to 350 degrees. The Prawns will need to be completely submerged in oil so you'll need at least 3 inches of oil, maybe more. Cook Prawns until golden brown, about 3 minutes.

 Note from Duke:

The heads and bodies of our Wild Mexican Prawns are removed at capture; this keeps the Prawn from degrading in flavor and texture. Immediately after, the Prawns are frozen, which preserves the freshness and crisp texture.

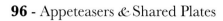

# MIGHTY MUSSELS "EL DUQUE"

Even though this dish has a Hispanic name, it is only that way because our Hispanic chefs dreamed it up. I think the people in Mexico would be very proud.

Serves two as an appeteaser

## Ingredients

14 Mussels de-bearded

1 tsp extra virgin olive oil

1 tsp fresh garlic, diced small

1 Tbsp Roasted Garlic Cloves (pg 328)

¼ cup heavy whipping cream

¼ cup Garlic Lover's Butter (pg 148), plus 1 Tbsp for bread

¼ cup North by Northwest Seafood Chowder Base (pg 160)

1 Tbsp fresh organic basil leaves, stems removed, diced small

½ tsp crushed red pepper

1 slice Essential Baking Company Rosemary Bread

## Directions

- In a sauté pan, heat olive oil on medium-high heat and briefly sauté garlic and Mussels (about 3 minutes). Do not brown garlic. Before cooking, discard any Mussels with open shells.

- Add cream, Garlic Lover's Butter, North by Northwest Seafood Chowder Base, basil and crushed red pepper. Boil uncovered until Mussels are just open and sauce has reduced by one-third.

- Meanwhile, toast, grill or broil rosemary bread and brush with Garlic Lover's Butter. Cut in quarters.

- Serve Mussels in a bowl with an extra bowl for the empties, and bread on the side for dipping. Discard Mussels that do not open after cooking.

## Penn Cove Mussels

*DukeWorthy™ Provider*

I used to look down on Mussels as something that grew on creosote pilings and couldn't possibly taste good. Had it not been for Peter Jefferds of Penn Cove Mussels, I would probably still think this. Back in 1977, he brought me a bucket of Mussels that he was experimenting with; in France, he had studied how to make Mussels grow on ropes beneath the docks and had set up a business using this method on Whidbey Island. I couldn't believe the amazing flavor, and Mussels have been on the menu ever since. Peter's sons, Ian and Raul, now own and operate Penn Cove Mussels. The Mussels are as good as ever and so is the Penn Cove ecosystem, which is thriving thanks to this tasty bivalve. The Monterey Bay Aquarium has identified them as "Super Green." "Wild" Bill and I have visited the Penn Cove Mussel rafts and have seen first-hand how the cool, clean waters of the farm raise sweet, plump Mussels unlike any other.

# CLAMMY FAYE CLAMS

Now here's a recipe with a little extra beverage for the chef...Washington Clams combined with fresh olive oil, garlic, roasted garlic, tomatoes, dill, butter and a touch of my favorite beer, Mac & Jacks African Amber combined with light beer. The good news: it only takes 3 tablespoons of each, so you can enjoy the rest of the refreshing beverages while you cook!

Serves two as an appeteaser

## Ingredients

2 cups fresh Washington Clams

1 tsp extra virgin olive oil

1 Tbsp fresh garlic, diced small

1½ tsp Roasted Garlic Cloves (pg 328)

1 Tbsp fresh tomatoes, diced small

pinch fresh organic dill, minced

pinch Duke's Ready Anytime Seasoning (pg 323)

3 Tbsp Mac & Jacks African Amber or your favorite beer

3 Tbsp Coors Light or your favorite light beer

2 Tbsp Garlic Lover's Butter (pg 148)

1 loaf Essential Baking Company Sourdough Bread for dipping, sliced in ¼-inch pieces

## Directions

• Heat olive oil in a sauté pan and sauté chopped garlic and Clams for 2 minutes. Before cooking, discard any Clams with open shells.

• Add roasted garlic, diced tomatoes, dill, Duke's Ready Anytime Seasoning, both beers and Garlic Lover's Butter.

• Bring liquid to boil. Cover and steam Clams until they perk and open.

• Serve Clams in their broth with the bread on the side for dipping. Discard Clams that do not open after cooking.

 Tips from Chef "Wild" Bill:

• Make sure the Clams are not too big. The small ones, about 1½ inches wide, are ideal.

• All fresh Clams are required by the health department to have "tags." These tags display not only the harvest date but the date they were delivered to the store or restaurant. Ask your local fishmongers when their Clams were harvested; if the date is past a week, keep shopping. Clams should have a clean scent with no open shells before they are cooked. If open before cooked, discard.

# DUNGENESS CRAB DIPPITY DOO

Fresh Dungeness Crab from the waters of Washington and Oregon that get the DukeWorthy™ Triple "S" mark—Sustainable, Sweet and Succulent. This recipe is for Crab lovers who like to splurge . . . okay, maybe it's a DukeWorthy™ Quadruple "S"!

Serves six as an appeteaser

## Ingredients

2 cups fresh Dungeness Crabmeat

¼ cup Walla Walla Sweet onions, minced

1 tsp extra virgin olive oil

¼ cup Make It Yourself Mayo (pg 320) or buy one made with olive oil

2 Tbsp sour cream

1 Tbsp Old Bay Seasoning

2 Tbsp Roasted Garlic Cloves (pg 328)

2 thick slices of creamy Havarti cheese, diced small

1 cup fresh spinach leaves, julienne-sliced small

3 six oz Essential Baking Company Sourdough Bread (round loaves)

6 Tbsp Garlic Lover's Butter (pg 148) for bread

6 slices Essential Baking Company Rosemary Bread

## Directions

• Squeeze all excess moisture from Crabmeat and refrigerate.

• Sauté sweet onions in olive oil; then transfer to a bowl and refrigerate.

• Combine Make It Yourself Mayo, sour cream, Old Bay Seasoning and roasted garlic in a food processor until smooth.

• Place spinach in a large mixing bowl and add ingredients from food processor, plus chopped onions, Havarti and Crab. Mix well.

• To make the bread bowls, slice top ½ inch from each round (reserve top for toasting and dipping). Then, with your fingers, pluck out the bread to create a hollow bowl.

• Scoop Crab mixture into the bread bowls and bake for 10-12 minutes at 350 degrees until just hot or until an internal thermometer reads 145 degrees (any hotter and it will start to separate). Alternately, you can bake in a shallow, oven-proof dish.

• Meanwhile, toast or broil rosemary bread and brush with Garlic Lover's Butter. Cut in quarters.

# HALIBUT KISSED CEVICHE gf

The key to the perfect ceviche is to use super-fresh or properly frozen fish. This is a dish native to Central and South America that uses lime juice to "cook" the fish, allowing the fish to retain its amazingly fresh flavor and not be influenced by heat from traditional cooking. Use Penny's Salsa Corn Tortilla Chips for dipping. They are the best I have ever tasted.

Serves four as an appeteaser

## Ingredients

8 oz Wild Alaska Halibut

juice of 3 limes

1 cup Dukecumber Pico de Gallo (pg 275)

2 Tbsp Guadalajara Guacamole (pg 276)

32 Penny's Salsa Corn Tortilla Chips

## Directions

- Fillet Halibut using the deep-skin method, which is to remove the gray matter along with the skin. If you are buying from your local fishmonger, ask to have the fillet deep-skinned as well. Be sure to remove all bones.

- Cut Halibut into ¼ inch pieces and mix with the lime juice. (The citric acid cooks the fish.)

- Cover and marinate overnight, stirring several times to ensure even cooking. (Halibut will lose all translucency when done.)

- Remove marinated Halibut pieces and discard liquid. Mix with Dukecumber Pico de Gallo. Serve in 2 large martini glasses with Penny's Salsa Corn Tortilla Chips on the side.

- Top with Guadalajara Guacamole.

 Tips from Chef "Wild" Bill:

- This is awesome on the deck on a hot day, but keep it refrigerated until just before serving. Colorful, healthy, and light, this is best when made ahead of time. This will free you up from cooking duties, so you can enjoy a libation with your guests. It is a great way to use up "trim" after you have filleted your catch of the day. We use Wild Alaska Halibut, but you can substitute almost any seafood, including Crab or Shrimp.

- Penny's Salsa Corn Tortilla Chips are gluten-free and made from corn, crispy and sturdy enough for dipping.

# SUPER CALAMARI STEAK STRIPS

Most restaurants serve the tentacles from smaller Squid, but you'll go wild for the steak-like texture of the larger ones. They are the *bartrami* species from the North Pacific. Chef "Wild" Bill tenderizes them in buttermilk, which also gives them a zesty, almost effervescent explosion of flavor.

Serves two as an appeteaser

## Ingredients

5 oz frozen Squid steak

2 Tbsp Darigold buttermilk

1 cup Baja Bandito Flour (pg 330)

GMO-free canola oil for frying

pinch fresh organic cilantro, stems removed, diced small

¼ cup Tickle Me Tequila Lime Aioli (pg 276)

**Optional ingredients**

¼ cup What's Up Wasabi Aioli (pg 321)

½ cup Duke's Coltrane Coleslaw (pg 280)

pinch fresh cilantro

## Directions

• Thaw Squid steaks in the refrigerator or under very cold running water. If they are not already tenderized, do so with a needling device (available in kitchen stores). If not already sliced, slice into ½ inch strips. Marinate in buttermilk for several hours. (The lactic acid in the buttermilk helps make the Squid tender.)

• Heat oil in a Dutch oven or thick-sided soup pot. The Squid will need to be completely submerged in oil so you'll need at least 3 inches of oil, maybe more. Heat oil to 350 degrees.

• Evenly coat Squid in Baja Bandito Flour.

• Fry until floating, about 1½ minutes; then transfer to a plate using a spiderweb ladle.

• Sprinkle with cilantro.

• Serve with Tickle Me Tequila Lime Aioli for dipping.

Tips from Chef "Wild" Bill:

• Caution: Use a candy or oil thermometer to check temperature and adjust slowly! If the oil is too hot, it will scorch the breading and the Squid will be undercooked. If the oil isn't hot enough, the breading will be soggy or fall off.

• For an extra flavor twist, serve with Duke's Coltrane Coleslaw and What's Up Wasabi Aioli.

# SURFER'S SURF CLAM STRIPS

Our Surf Clams, which hail from the East Coast near Martha's Vineyard, have the clean fragrance of the ocean. The sweet and salty flavor lingers in your mouth long after each bite.

Serves two as an appeteaser

## Ingredients

5 oz sliced Surf Clams or Razor Clams

2 Tbsp Darigold buttermilk

1 cup Baja Bandito Flour (pg 330)

GMO-free canola oil for frying

¼ cup Tickle Me Tequila Lime Aioli (pg 276)

¼ cup What's Up Wasabi Aioli (pg 321)

¼ cup Duke's Coltrane Coleslaw (pg 280)

 Tip from Chef "Wild" Bill:

Caution: Use a candy or oil thermometer to check the temperature and adjust oil temperature slowly! If the oil is too hot, it will scorch the breading and the Clams will be undercooked. If the oil isn't hot enough, the breading will be soggy or fall off.

## Directions

- Thaw Surf or Razor Clams in the refrigerator if frozen or under very cold running water. If they are not already tenderized, do so with a needling device (available from kitchen stores). Otherwise, the Clams will be too tough. If not pre-sliced, slice into ½ inch strips.

- Place Clams in a bowl with buttermilk and marinate for several hours or overnight. (The lactic acid helps make the Clam strips tender.)

- Remove Clam strips from buttermilk and toss in Baja Bandito Flour, coating evenly.

- Heat oil in a Dutch oven or very thick-sided soup pot. The Clams must be completely submerged in oil, so you'll need 3 inches, maybe more. Heat oil to 330 to 350 degrees.

- Fry in small batches until floating, about 1½ minutes, and transfer to a plate using a spiderweb ladle.

- Serve with Duke's Coltrane Coleslaw and the two aiolis for dipping. If desired, garnish with fresh chopped parsley and serve with fresh lemon slices.

# Sumptuous Salads

For a fit, healthy body.

# PLENTY OF IRON SPINACH SALAD gf

This timeless classic has been on our menu nearly unchanged for thirty-eight years. It's just as current today as it was then. It's a huge favorite. Plus, spinach makes you strong. The recipe is actually old enough to be inspired by Popeye himself. People still know who he is, right? It has plenty of olive oil in it; extra virgin olive oil though, not Popeye's girlfriend.

Serves one as an entrée or two as a starter

## Ingredients

4 oz organic baby spinach, fresh and local when available

¼ cup Sweet and Secret Caper Vinaigrette (pg 137)

1 hard-boiled cage-free egg (see How To Boil An Egg, pg 326), diced medium

1 Tbsp Parmesan and 1 Tbsp Asiago cheese, grated and combined

2 Tbsp fresh tomatoes, diced

2 Tbsp blanched slivered almonds, roasted (bake raw blanched slivered almonds in a 350 degree oven for 7 minutes or until golden brown)

2 slices nitrite-free bacon, cooked crispy and diced medium

## Directions

- In a large bowl, toss spinach leaves with Sweet and Secret Caper Vinaigrette. Top with egg, cheese, tomatoes, almonds and chopped bacon.

 Tips from Chef "Wild" Bill:

- Buy fresh local spinach from your farmer's market in summer or search for pre-washed and bagged organic spinach in your grocery store. Make sure to double or triple wash your spinach; dirt likes to hide in it. I recommend even washing bagged spinach. Also, smaller leaves are more tender.

- Try it with our Blackened Wild Alaska Salmon on top.

# ORGANIC WILD CHILD MIXED GREENS gf

This salad was our first foray into the world of organic vegetables nearly 12 years ago when organic produce first started becoming readily available and more affordable, and it has since become a family favorite. Our goal is to serve 100 percent organic food, and we get closer to that target every year.

Serves one as an entrée or two as a starter

## Ingredients

1½ cups organic field greens

14 Amy's Candied Pecans (pg 139)

6 fresh grapefruit sections

6 fresh orange sections

2 Tbsp bleu cheese crumbles (we use Roth brand "Buttermilk Blue")

¼ cup Carry On Tarragon Vinaigrette (pg 134)

## Directions

• Toss greens with Carry On Tarragon Vinaigrette in a large salad bowl. Top with grapefruit and orange sections, bleu cheese crumbles and pecans.

 Tips from Chef "Wild" Bill:

• Our Nothing But Blue Sky Bleu Cheese Dressing is gluten-free because the Roth brand "Buttermilk Blue" is not grown on bread like most other bleu cheese.

• Go for organic greens whenever possible and make your own dressings for the freshest, most delicious flavors. And keep it natural—stay away from ingredients (when you read the label) that you can't pronounce.

# SWEET BLACKBERRY WEDGE SALAD  gf

I've always liked bleu cheese with berries of all kinds. This fruity spin on a wedge brings fruit flavors that combine beautifully with the savory taste of bacon. It really is something special. This salad is also delightful with fresh raspberries, strawberries, cherries or blueberries.

Serves one

## Ingredients

¼ head iceberg lettuce, washed and cut into quarters

1 Tbsp bleu cheese crumbles

2 Tbsp tomatoes, diced

1 slice nitrite-free bacon, cooked crispy and diced medium

1 Tbsp slivered almonds, toasted (bake raw blanched slivered almonds in a 350 degree oven for 7 minutes or until golden brown)

6 Tbsp Nothing But Blue Sky Bleu Cheese Dressing (pg 139)

7 fresh blackberries

## Directions

• Sprinkle bleu cheese crumbles, tomatoes, bacon and almonds over the quartered lettuce. Then drizzle with bleu cheese dressing and top with blackberries. Also good with other fresh berries.

 Tip from Chef "Wild" Bill:

Almonds taste fresher when you toast them yourself.

## "Eat Your Greens!"

# GRASS-FED "FOOL AROUND & FALL IN LOVE" FILET MIGNON SALAD gf

For some reason, this salad is a favorite of our women guests. Maybe it's the iron; maybe it's the omega-3s in the grass-fed beef. Maybe it's the flavor of the natural, grass-fed beef itself. At any rate, you don't find this on too many menus, but it's a really healthy version of steak and salad.

Serves one as an entrée or two as a starter

## Ingredients

3 cups organic wild mixed greens

14 Amy's Candied Pecans (pg 139)

6 fresh grapefruit sections

6 fresh orange sections

4 Tbsp bleu cheese crumbles
(we use Roth brand "Buttermilk Blue")

¼ cup Carry On Tarragon Vinaigrette
(pg 134)

8 oz grass-fed filet

Pinch Duke's Ready Anytime Seasoning
(pg 323)

## Directions

• Sprinkle Duke's Ready Anytime Seasoning on top and bottom of filet.

• Broil filet, approximately 5 minutes per side, depending on desired doneness.

• Toss greens with Carry On Tarragon Vinaigrette in a large salad bowl. Top with grapefruit and orange sections, bleu cheese crumbles and Amy's Candied Pecans.

• Slice filet in 8 slices and fan out over salad.

 Tip from Chef "Wild" Bill:
Our Nothing But Blue Sky Bleu Cheese Dressing is gluten-free because the Roth brand "Buttermilk Blue" is not grown on bread like most other bleu cheese.

# ALL HAIL CAESAR SALAD

When Caesar Cardini created what later became known as the Caesar Salad, he claimed it came out of pure need, maybe even desperation. In 1924, after a big rush of business depleted his restaurant's kitchen supplies, Caesar was forced to improvise. He served his creation as a finger-food (maybe he had run out of forks as well) with whole lettuce leaves drizzled with dressing made from coddled eggs and Italian olive oil. Duke's has made some improvements over the years to give this classic more flavor (like adding fresh garlic; it just isn't a Caesar without it) making this an official Duke's favorite.

Serves one as an entrée or two as a starter

## Ingredients

3 cups fresh romaine lettuce hearts, chopped 1-inch wide, washed and spun dry

14 Duke's Crunchy Croutons (pg 328)

6 Tbsp All Hail Caesar Salad Dressing (pg136)

2 Tbsp Parmesan cheese and 2 Tbsp Asiago cheese, grated and mixed well

## Directions

• Keep chopped and spun romaine refrigerated until just before serving. Toss with dressing, Duke's Crunchy Croutons and half the cheeses. Sprinkle with remaining cheese just before serving. For an additional taste treat, serve with Blackened Salmon (below).

# BLACKENED WILD ALASKA SALMON CAESAR SALAD

## Ingredients

8 oz fillet of Wild Alaska Salmon

1 tsp Blackening Spice Of Life (pg 323)

1 Tbsp Let's Be Clarified Butter (pg 148)

## Directions

• Dredge one side of Salmon in Blackening Spice. Melt Let's Be Clarified Butter in a sauté pan or on a flat griddle, and cook Salmon until caramelized (3-4 minutes per side or until fish has lost all its translucency).

# OUT OF THE BLEU CAESAR SALAD — This is "Duke's Way"

Technically, it's not a true Caesar without "Caesar" dressing, but we're not really into technicalities at Duke's. Truth be told, I personally LOVE this combination, so here's a short, quick and easy spin on a Caesar that is literally out of the bleu . . . or rather blue, no bleu . . . straight from me, the actual Duke, rather than the entity that is Duke's. Don't worry; sometimes, I get them confused, too. We both wear a lot of checkered blue, or was it bleu? Substitute Nothing But Blue Sky Bleu Cheese Dressing (pg 139). I even add sliced avocado and sliced tomatoes. Enjoy.

# I HEAR THE OCEAN FRESH SALAD gf

The inspiration for this dish originated from one of my favorite Seattle restaurants, Shuckers, located in the Fairmont Hotel. I ordered this hauntingly delicious dish for years without being able to figure out its unique, mysterious flavor. I've always prided myself on being able to figure out just about any flavor in a dish and what makes it stand out. Finally, one night Chef "Wild" Bill and I ordered it and begged the waiter for the answer. The mystery ingredient . . . tarragon. It was perfectly disguised in combination with the other ingredients and brought this salad together in the most perfect way.

Serves one as an entrée or two as a starter

## Ingredients

5 medium Wild Mexican Prawns (21 to 25 to the lb), peeled and deveined

6 Tbsp Why Not Take Olive Me & Herb Marinade (pg 138)

½ cup iceberg lettuce, diced small

½ cup Napa cabbage, diced small

¼ cup Dukecumber Pico de Gallo (pg 275)

¼ fresh avocado, diced small

2 Tbsp bleu cheese crumbles

6 Tbsp Ocean Fresh Dressing (pg 135)

¼ cup fresh Dungeness Crabmeat

large pinch fresh organic parsley, diced small

## Directions

• Marinate Prawns in Why Not Take Olive Me & Herb Marinade for 3 hours in the refrigerator.

• Toss iceberg lettuce, Napa cabbage, Dukecumber Pico de Gallo, avocado and bleu cheese with Ocean Fresh dressing.

• Broil marinated Prawns for 2-3 minutes per side and add to salad along with fresh Dungeness Crab. (Reserve a whole Maris leg and place on top for a real wow!) Sprinkle with parsley.

# "UN"CHOPPED SEAFOOD SALAD gf

If you like seafood, this is the salad for you. We call it "Un"Chopped because we don't chop up the ingredients like a traditional Chopped. To make it more confusing, I like to chop up the "Un"Chopped so I am guaranteed a taste of seafood in every bite. This is the ultimate seafood version of a Chopped salad with large Wild Alaska Weathervane Scallops and Wild Mexican Prawns. This salad is a showstopper. Yes, it's that good.

Serves one as an entrée or two as a starter

## Ingredients

3 Wild Mexican Prawns (size 21-25 per lb), peeled and deveined

3 Wild Alaska Weathervane Scallops (size 20-30 Scallops per lb)

⅓ cup Why Not Take Olive Me & Herb Marinade (pg 138)

4 romaine lettuce leaf hearts, diced small

½ cup Napa cabbage, sliced into ribbons

¼ cup roasted cashews

¼ cup tomato, diced medium

¼ avocado, diced medium

¼ cup crumbled Feta cheese

¼ cup Duke's Sinful Citrus Vinaigrette (pg 138)

## Directions

• Using two parallel skewers, bisect one Scallop, followed by one Prawn, matching the natural curve of the Shrimp so it hugs the top edge of the Scallop below it. Add another Scallop and Prawn in this way until all 6 pieces are flat and nested.

• Marinate in Why Not Take Olive Me & Herb Marinade for at least 2 hours in the refrigerator. (Be patient with the marinade; it takes time to incorporate the yummy flavors.)

• On a hot flat griddle or large sauté pan, cook Scallops and Prawns on their skewer until golden brown, approximately 2-3 minutes per side.

• In a mixing bowl, place salad greens, cashews, tomatoes, avocado and Feta, and toss with Duke's Sinful Citrus Vinaigrette. Top with Scallop & Prawn Skewer.

# BLACKENED WILD ALASKA SALMON TY COBB gf

Ty Cobb played baseball a little differently and a lot better than nearly everyone. We like to think that our Cobb is a lot like Ty. The Alaska Salmon and Blackening Spice Of Life adds a flavor twist you'll never forget. We like to think Ty would approve as well.

Serves one as an entrée or two as a starter

## Ingredients

8 oz Wild Alaska Salmon

1 tsp Blackening Spice Of Life (pg 323)

1 Tbsp Let's Be Clarified Butter (pg 148)

3 cups fresh romaine hearts, chopped

¼ cup Nothing But Blue Sky Bleu Cheese Dressing (pg 139)

2 slices nitrite-free bacon, cooked and chopped into 1-inch pieces

¼ cup fresh tomatoes, diced

1 hard-boiled cage-free egg (see How To Boil An Egg, pg 326), diced medium

¼ cup bleu cheese crumbles (we use Roth brand "Buttermilk Blue")

¼ fresh avocado, sliced and fanned

## Directions

• Fillet Salmon using the deep-skin method, which is to remove the gray matter along with the skin and pluck the pin bones with needle-nose pliers or boning tweezers. If you are buying from your local fishmonger, ask to have the fillet deep-skinned as well.

• Dredge one side of Salmon in Blackening Spice Of Life. (Don't worry; doing only one side provides plenty of heat.)

• Sauté Salmon in a pan or on a flat griddle in Let's Be Clarified Butter until caramelized, approximately 3-4 minutes per side.

• Toss romaine with Nothing But Blue Sky Bleu Cheese Dressing in a large salad bowl.

• Create four side-by-side rows on top of the salad with bacon, tomatoes, egg and bleu cheese crumbles. Top with fanned avocado and piping-hot Salmon.

 Tip from Chef "Wild" Bill:

Try this salad with chicken for a true grilled chicken cobb salad.

# DUNGENESS CRAB "UN" CAKE SALAD

The Hideaway Golf Club in Palm Desert serves frozen grapes at the end of the 9th hole where players are given this sweet, refreshing treat. One time while golfing there, I thought, "These could be the key to an amazing salad!" This amazing salad then became our very own Dungeness Crab "Un"Cake Salad.

Serves one

## Ingredients

1 Dungeness Crab "Un"Cake (pg 238)

12 frozen seedless red grapes

2 Tbsp pumpkin seeds, toasted

pinch Duke's Ready Anytime Seasoning (pg 323)

½ tsp extra virgin olive oil

2 cups organic field greens

3 Tbsp Sinful Citrus Vinaigrette (pg 138)

2 small (2 Tbsp) wheels goat cheese (we use Laura Chenel brand)

## Directions

• Wash grapes and remove stems. Drain off excess water. Place on a sheet pan in a single layer, not touching each other, in the freezer. Once frozen, transfer to a container and continue to store frozen.

• Toss pumpkin seeds in olive oil with Duke's Ready Anytime Seasoning and place on a cookie sheet. Bake at 350 degrees until golden brown. Allow to cool and then cover and store at room temperature.

• Toss organic field greens in Sinful Citrus Vinaigrette, evenly coating all the leaves, and place on a chilled plate. Top with goat cheese wheels, frozen grapes, toasted pumpkin seeds and a Dungeness Crab "Un"Cake.

 Tip from Chef "Wild" Bill:

Make extra grapes and enjoy them as a healthy dessert. I like to munch on them at home while watching a movie. In the kitchen at Duke's, frozen grapes are a precious delicacy.

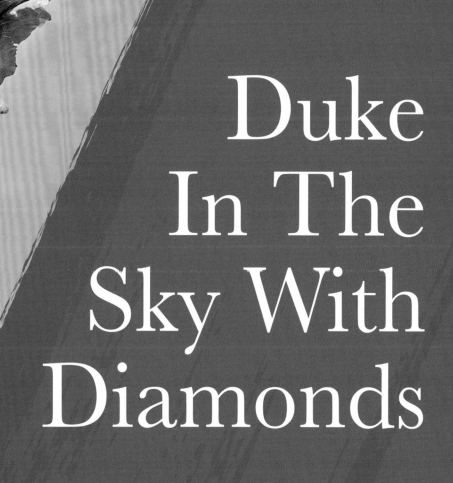

# Duke
# In The
# Sky With
# Diamonds

# Delectable Dressings & Amy's Candied Pecans

## "It's really all about the condiments, isn't it?"

# CARRY ON TARRAGON VINAIGRETTE gf

Tarragon is by far my favorite herb and brings a mysterious and haunting flavor to everything it encounters. Your guests will be pleasantly puzzled by the unique tastes that come out of everything you cook with this tantalizing herb.

Makes enough for 25 entrée size salads

## Ingredients

6 Tbsp sweet onions, diced small

3 Tbsp fresh garlic, diced small

6 Tbsp sugar in the raw

2 Tbsp kosher salt

1 tsp white pepper

6 Tbsp Dijon mustard

6 Tbsp high-quality balsamic vinegar

6 Tbsp red wine vinegar

4 cups extra virgin olive oil

1 Tbsp dried tarragon

## Directions

• Purée onions, garlic, sugar, salt and pepper in food processor until smooth.

• Add vinegars and Dijon mustard, and mix for 30 seconds.

• While blades are running, slowly add olive oil in a thin stream until it emulsifies.

• Add tarragon and mix for 30 seconds.

 Tips from Chef "Wild" Bill:

• Extra virgin olive oil does not store well in the refrigerator. It solidifies. If you are making this for refrigerated storage for later use, substitute a blend of equal parts extra virgin olive oil and salad oil.

• This recipe is purposely larger because small batches often separate, and with no eggs, the emulsification is on the challenging side.

# OCEAN FRESH DRESSING gf

This sauce is as fresh as the ocean, complete with a refreshing salty finish.

Makes enough for approximately 5 entrée size salads

## Ingredients

1 cup Make It Yourself Mayo (pg 320) or buy one made with olive oil

6 Tbsp Darigold buttermilk

2 Tbsp sweet onions, diced small

1 Tbsp fresh garlic, diced small

1 Tbsp fresh organic parsley, stems removed, diced small

1 Tbsp fresh organic basil leaves, diced small

1 Tbsp green onion, green parts only, diced small

2 tsp dried tarragon

pinch black pepper

pinch kosher salt

## Directions

• Purée onion, garlic and fresh herbs in a food processor.

• Combine Make It Yourself Mayo and buttermilk in a mixing bowl.

• Add tarragon, pepper and salt. Whisk until smooth.

# ALL HAIL CAESAR SALAD DRESSING gf

Ultimately, Julius Caesar's fall from grace was too much power. In order to make sure your dressing is balanced just right and doesn't follow the fate of Julius, keep in mind the following keys to perfecting this dressing:

• Plenty of garlic (but not too much); it needs to sing to you, not punch you in the face.

• Anchovies add a special flavor that makes the taste of this dressing unique. If you don't like the taste of anchovies, add 1 Tbsp of salt.

• Just the right amount of lemon. You barely want to detect it.

Makes enough for approximately 6 entrée size salads

## Ingredients

2 organic eggs

1 ¼ cups extra virgin olive oil

1 Tbsp Dijon Mustard

2 Tbsp freshly squeezed lemon juice

3 Tbsp raspberry vinegar

1 ½ Tbsp white wine vinegar

2 Tbsp granulated garlic

½ tsp white pepper

½ tsp Lea & Perrins Worcestershire Sauce

½ tsp kosher salt

2 Tbsp fresh garlic, diced small

2 anchovy fillets or 2 Tbsp anchovy paste

1 ½ Tbsp Parmesan cheese and 1 ½ Tbsp Asiago cheese, grated and combined

## Directions

• Place eggs in a food processor and mix until frothy, about 3 minutes. While mixing, add oils very slowly in a steady, small stream until just emulsified. Pulse in remaining ingredients. Store covered and refrigerated.

• Option: Add a dash of Tabasco to taste.

# SWEET AND SECRET CAPER VINAIGRETTE gf

The key to a successful menu is two-fold: let it evolve but keep a good base of favorites. You want to keep your guests trying new things, but don't be afraid to keep a favorite on the menu. We've been making this dressing at Duke's since we opened because, well, it's really that good. Sometimes you need to honor what works well for the guest, and that's just what we have done—continue to serve this favorite.

Makes enough dressing for 12 entrée size salads

## Ingredients

3 organic eggs (liquid pasteurized can be used)

1 cup extra virgin olive oil

3 Tbsp fresh-squeezed lemon juice

2 Tbsp capers

1 Tbsp dry mustard powder

1 tsp black pepper

1 tsp granulated garlic

1 tsp kosher salt

½ cup sugar

¼ cup Organic or All Natural Heinz Ketchup (make your own or purchase one with no high fructose corn syrup)

½ cup red wine vinegar

## Directions

• Place eggs in a food processor and beat until light and frothy, about 3 minutes. While mixing, slowly add the oil in a steady, small stream. Pulse in remaining ingredients until fully incorporated.

 Tip from Chef "Wild" Bill:

Extra virgin olive oil does not store well in the refrigerator. It solidifies. If you are making this for refrigerated storage for later use, substitute a blend of equal parts extra virgin olive oil and salad oil.

# SINFUL CITRUS VINAIGRETTE gf

The citrus flavors in this beautifully balanced vinaigrette deliver a taste so delicious you'd swear that it's bad for you. Lemons are naturally rich in Vitamin D and are packed with flavor, making this dressing the perfect complement to any salad.

Makes enough for 6 entrée size salads

## Ingredients

1 organic egg

2 Tbsp fresh whole garlic cloves

2 Tbsp fresh organic basil leaves, stems removed

¾ tsp kosher salt

1½ tsp fresh cracked black pepper

1 cup + 2 Tbsp extra virgin olive oil

¼ cup fresh squeezed lemon juice

## Directions

• Place egg in a food processor and blend for 2 minutes until frothy. While mixing, blend in garlic and basil until smooth. Add salt and pepper. In a thin, constant stream, slowly add olive oil (too fast and the dressing will separate). Add lemon juice and mix just until smooth.

 Tip from Chef "Wild" Bill:

Extra virgin olive oil does not store well in the refrigerator. It solidifies. If you are making this for refrigerated storage for later use, substitute a blend of equal parts extra virgin olive oil and salad oil.

# WHY NOT TAKE OLIVE ME & HERB MARINADE gf

Your taste buds will be dancing to Frank Sinatra in this delicious ensemble of olive oil, herbs, spices and garlic.

Makes enough to marinate 5 Scallop & Prawn Skewers

## Ingredients

1 cup extra virgin olive oil

¼ cup Duke's Superb Herb Blend (pg 322)

1 Tbsp Duke's Ready Anytime Seasoning (pg 323)

1 Tbsp fresh organic parsley, stems removed, diced small

2 Tbsp fresh garlic, diced small

## Directions

• Mix all ingredients together and refrigerate for at least 4 hours.

 Tip from Chef "Wild" Bill:

This marinade adds flavor and a fresh taste to seafood without being overwhelming. Try it with grilled Prawns, grilled fish or even chicken. If broiling, make sure to drain off any excess oil to avoid a flame-up.

# NOTHING BUT BLUE SKY BLEU CHEESE DRESSING gf

This family favorite is so beloved by my crew that we could eat it for breakfast and often do. It's mild enough for people who don't like strong-smelling cheeses but bold enough for those who enjoy the unique taste of Roquefort (bleu cheese made from goat's milk).

Makes enough for 17 entrée size salads

## Ingredients

¼ cup sweet onions, diced small

1 Tbsp fresh garlic, diced small

1 cup Darigold buttermilk

6 Tbsp sour cream

5 Tbsp red wine vinegar

1 Tbsp Lea & Perrins Worcestershire Sauce

2 Tbsp fresh ground pepper

4 cups Make It Yourself Mayo (pg 320) or buy one made with olive oil

½ tsp kosher salt

5 Tbsp bleu cheese crumbles (we use Roth brand "Buttermilk Blue" which is gluten-free)

## Directions

• In a mini-food processor, chop onion and garlic to a fine paste.

• Scrape into a bowl and add the rest of the ingredients except bleu cheese. Mix until incorporated.

• Fold in bleu cheese. Do not over-mix. Refrigerate in a covered container.

 Tip from Chef "Wild" Bill:

Our Nothing But Blue Sky Bleu Cheese Dressing is also gluten-free because the Roth brand "Buttermilk Blue" is not grown on bread like most other bleu cheese.

# AMY'S CANDIED PECANS gf

My daughter Amy has made these as gifts during the holidays for years. I love them so much that mine are gone before Christmas. As I was eating them one holiday, I thought, "Man, these would taste amazing on a salad." Amy taught our chefs how to make them, and now I don't have to wait until December for this sweet and savory treat. They are great for a snack when you need a little reward for being good.

## Ingredients

½ cup brown sugar

¼ cup water

1 lb pecan halves

2 tsp pumpkin pie spice

## Directions

• Mix sugar and water in a heavy saucepan and heat on medium, stirring often, until sugar is dissolved. Set aside to cool.

• Mix pecans into sugar water and place on a sheet pan lined with parchment paper.

• Bake in a 350-degree oven for 10 minutes. Remove from oven and dust with pumpkin pie spice, tossing evenly to coat.

# Double Sourdough Bread

"People drive across town for our piping hot sourdough bread just out of the oven."

# Our Very Own Baker Makes Our Double Sourdough

Duke's just wouldn't be Duke's without our famous double sourdough bread. I fell in love with sourdough many years ago while training to be a stockbroker in San Francisco. It has the perfect combination of a crispy, blistered crust and a soft, sour inside that brings together a mouth-watering experience. When we opened our first Duke's in 1977, I introduced that same perfect sourdough to Seattle's diners. I worked with a well-known Seattle bakery to perfect the formula that later became known as Seattle Sourdough. Today, it is made especially to our DukeWorthy™ standards. Essential Baking Company bakes it fresh every day, just for you. Founder and baker, George DePasquale, has a passion for excellent bread that stems from his childhood. He honed his skills in San Francisco and later moved to Seattle where he eventually developed the largest artisan bakery in the

city. George and Essential really understand how to make sourdough. Their bakers "get it." Essential shares our philosophy about wholesome, all-natural ingredients. Duke's is very demanding when it comes to quality, flavor, and recipe adherence. Essential delivers with wild yeast, hearth-baked ovens and USDA organic ingredients. Essential has become, well, essential to Duke's.

## To Build A Sourdough Starter:

The following recipe comes from our baker friends at The Essential Baking Company. If you already have an active and healthy sourdough starter, you can use that in the recipe that follows. Otherwise, you'll need to get a starter going. It's not hard, but it will take about a week.

**Day 1**: Mix 1 cup of flour and 1¼ cups of cool water in a medium-sized bowl. Mix the two ingredients just until they come together. Cover with a towel or plastic wrap and let stand at room temperature.

**Day 2**: Remove 1 cup of the starter and discard it. (It seems odd, but it needs to be made with the larger amounts, though in the end, only about ½ is needed.) Add ½ cup cool water and ½ cup flour to the remaining starter and mix just until it comes together. Repeat this process for days 3, 4, 5 and 6. Your starter should become more bubbly and alive day by day. On the seventh day, it will be ready to use.

**If you want to keep your starter going:** On Day 7, remove a cup of the starter, but save it and put it aside this time. This will be the starter you'll use in your bread. (If you're not going to bake, discard it.) Follow the directions from Day 2. Cover and let your starter stand at room temperature for 3 hours. Now you can put it into the refrigerator. You'll still need to feed it about once a month (minimum), using the instructions from Day 2 to keep it alive. When it's time to feed your starter, remove it from the refrigerator and let it stand at room temperature for about 2 hours. Then follow the directions from Day 2.

## For the Bread:

### Ingredients

- 6 cups bread flour
- 3 cups lukewarm water
- 1 tablespoon salt
- ½ teaspoon rapid rise yeast
- 1 cup of sourdough starter

### Directions

**If you are mixing by hand:**

- Combine all the ingredients in a large bowl just until it all comes together. Turn it out on the table and knead for 12 minutes.

**If you are mixing in a mixer:**

- Combine all the ingredients in the bowl of the mixer, fitted with the dough hook, and mix for 4 minutes on slow, then 6 minutes on fast. Cover and let rest for 30 minutes.

**After mixing:**

- Let the dough rise at room temp about 2 hours or until you can leave an indentation with your finger. The dough should rise until it is 1½ times its original volume.
- Divide the dough in half. Gently press the gas out of each piece, and shape each piece into a ball.
- Allow the loaves to rise until about 1 hour or 1½ times the original volume.
- Pre-heat the oven to 450°. If you have a baking stone, preheat the stone along with the oven.
- With a spritzer, spray the inside of the oven with water every minute or so for the first 10 minutes.
- Bake the loaves for 35-40 minutes or until they are golden brown.

# Bountiful Butters

You butter believe it.

# "HOLIDAYS" HOLLANDAISE SAUCE gf

When my daughter Amy was little, she couldn't say the word, "Hollandaise." She called it "Holidays" sauce, and it will forever be so in my heart.

Makes enough for 6 portions

## Ingredients

3 organic eggs

½ cup unsalted Darigold butter, melted

1 tsp fresh lemon juice

pinch of sea salt

pinch of white pepper

pinch of cayenne pepper or a dash of Tabasco sauce

 Tip from Chef "Wild" Bill:
This sauce is great with eggs for a Benedict or a "Beneduke" (with Crab and spinach).

## Directions

- Make a double boiler by filling a saucepan halfway full of water and heat until almost boiling.

- Separate the yolks from the whites, and place the yolks in a stainless steel bowl. The bowl should rest on top of the saucepan without touching the water.

- Whisk egg yolks by hand to frothing while they are heating, to about 120 degrees. (Be careful not to overheat or you'll end up with scrambled eggs! If this happens, eat them with a glass of pinot noir and start over.)

- Whisk in lemon juice.

- You'll need help with this next step: While whisking, ask a friend/family member/guest to add butter in a slow, steady stream. This will emulsify the ingredients into a silky, smooth sauce.

- Add salt and white pepper. Then add cayenne pepper or Tabasco.

Note from Duke:

I never bought in to the "butter is bad for you" phase in cooking. Butter always tasted great to me, and the scientific theories just didn't have the ring of truth. Besides, I really disliked the taste of margarine. Now, all of us Butter Believers are vindicated. And Darigold makes it easy with an all natural and smooth, silky taste. You Butter Believe It!

# COMPOUND TASTY HERB BUTTER gf

As the folks at Darigold have always said, "Butter is for Lovers," and boy, is it! I love butter on anything and everything, and Chef "Wild" Bill has created a perfect butter blend.

Makes enough for 30 1-inch coins

## Ingredients

½ lb Darigold butter (2 sticks), softened

juice from 1 lemon

¼ cup Roasted Garlic Cloves (pg 328)

¼ bunch fresh organic parsley, stems removed, diced small

6 Tbsp Duke's Superb Herb Blend (pg 322)

2 Tbsp fresh organic basil leaves, stems removed, diced small

## Directions

• Blend Darigold butter in a food processor until soft.

• Slowly add lemon juice until combined.

• Add remaining ingredients until fully incorporated. Scrape sides with rubber spatula and mix again.

• To store, make a roll the diameter of a fifty-cent piece and wrap in parchment paper; then refrigerate or freeze. Slice small "coins" off of the roll as needed. Keep frozen for later use.

### Tip from Chef "Wild" Bill:

This butter adds a gourmet touch to broiled potatoes or asparagus. Try tarragon or lemon basil for a delicious twist.

# LET'S BE CLARIFIED BUTTER gf

Clarified butter is simply butter with the milk solids removed. Chefs like it because of its clean, buttery flavor, and it doesn't burn as easily as regular butter.

- Slowly melt Darigold butter in a heavy-gauge pan. Skim the white foam off the top with a spoon. (Reserve it if you like buttery popcorn; see tip below).

- Boil Darigold butter for about 1 minute. When the milk solids on the bottom of the pan begin to brown, slowly pour through cheesecloth, leaving the brown specks in the bottom of the pan. Refrigerate or freeze.

 Tips from Chef "Wild" Bill:

- Drizzle the white foam from the top of the melted butter over popcorn for a salty, buttery crunch. Or serve it melted over homemade Belgian waffles.

- Duke's buys butter, milk, cream and buttermilk from local producer Darigold, which has no rBGH (bovine growth hormone also known as bovine somatotropin or rBST). Darigold butter is the best you can get. Darigold has a European Vacuum Churn that removes most of the air out of the butter (its butter contains less than .5 percent air while other butter contains 5-6 percent). When clarifying Darigold butter, all of the fat solids sink to the bottom, leaving nothing but glorious pure ghee (clarified butter) on top, making it extremely easy to separate.

# GARLIC LOVER'S BUTTER gf

It's simple, but oh, so tasty, on just about everything. It's especially good with Essential Baking Company Rosemary Bread, in pastas and with barbecued Wild Salmon.

1 lb Darigold butter, softened

¼ cup fresh garlic, diced small

3 Tbsp fresh organic parsley, stems removed, diced small

- Whip butter until double in volume. Add garlic and parsley until fully incorporated. Refrigerate or freeze.

# FILL ME UP BUTTERCUP BUTTA CREAM SAUCE gf

Chef "Wild" Bill created this cream-and-butter sauce that's just as tasty as "Holidays" sauce without as much pomp and circumstance. Making "Holidays" Sauce is no simple task. Fill Me Up Buttercup Butta Cream Sauce is somewhat easier to prepare.

Makes 1 cup (enough for 6 servings)

## Ingredients

1 cup heavy whipping cream

½ cup unsalted Darigold butter

juice of one lemon

## Directions

- Place cream in a heavy-bottomed stockpot and reduce on medium heat by half of its original volume. Maintain temperature between 80 and 100 degrees and slowly whisk in unsalted butter. Add lemon juice. Continue to hold between 80 and 100 degrees. If it gets too hot, it will break. If it gets too cold, it will solidify.

 Tip from Chef "Wild" Bill:

Cream with the highest amount of butterfat will make your sauce rich and silky. Ultra-pasteurized cream doesn't reduce as well and has a flat flavor.


# I LOVE HAZELNUT BUTTA CREAM SAUCE gf

This is a wonderful version of a sweet cream sauce. It's a dreamy combination that harkens back to the butterscotch sundaes I loved as a kid.

- Follow the recipe for Fill Me Up Buttercup Butta Cream Sauce (pg 149) and add ¼ cup Hazelnut syrup along with the lemon juice.

 Tip from Chef "Wild" Bill:

Hazelnut syrup can be found at most coffee shops. Try asking your neighborhood barista for some or visiting your local Cash & Carry or Restaurant Supply store.

# THE BUTTER THAT
# *melts you*

I asked the folks at Darigold to write about their experience with Duke's Chowder House. Here's what they said:

"Darigold does dairy differently. Since 1918, the company has been a farmer-owned dairy co-op, folding the tenets of good farming practices right into their butter, milk, and cream. Family farms tend the cows that make our products—and those hard-working girls sure can melt your heart.

"It was our butter that melted Duke's heart. Based on his Darigold experience at other restaurants, he opened Duke's Chowder House in 1977 with Darigold's butter and cream in the kitchen. He's a passionate butter lover—why else would he devote an entire cookbook chapter to butters?—and he wants to make sure his customers, who start every Duke's experience with that golden spread on hot sourdough rolls, get the very best.

"Today, his Award Winning Clam Chowder, which uses both butter and cream, is the cornerstone of his business: He serves more than 245,000 cups and 105,000 bowls of that Chowder each year, plus about 15,000 cups and 35,000 bowls of Lobster Mobster Pernod Chowder, Ragin' Cajun Chicken Corn Chowder, and Crabby Baby Bisque, combined. He prizes Darigold's consistency, and loves the products' natural, creamy flavor. And because butter and cream have been such an important part of his restaurant's journey, he wants his customers to know he trusts Darigold. 'It's the butter that melts you,' we like to say. We're glad Duke agrees."

**FUN FACT:** If you cooked every recipe in this book, you'd use 8.97 pounds of **Darigold butter.**

# Champion Chowders

Brought to you by the Seattle Chowder Cook-Off Champ (that would be Duke's) three years in a row.

# The Chowder That Changed Duke's World

My grandfather, John Fitzgerald Cox, who bragged that his Clam Chowder was the best in all of New England, was the inspiration for our Chowder. Actually, I remember his Chowder being very brothy with too much Clam taste for my liking, so maybe it was his effort, or rather, his confidence that inspired me to make the best Chowder on the planet.

Grampa was determined to keep the reputation of his Chowder bowls being empty at every serving (obviously, you can't brag about your Chowder being the best if bowls weren't empty), so he would always put a plate of fresh chocolate éclairs in the middle of the table. This made it clear that my ticket to enjoying one was an empty Chowder bowl. So, after countless years and bowls of Chowder, I more or less acquired a taste for Clams. When Duke's opened, I decided to tackle Grampa Cox's Chowder recipe and truly make it the best, if not in all of New England, surely in all of Seattle, or what the heck, the best in the world! I wanted Duke's Chowder to have a distinct fresh herb flavor and creamy texture with a fragrant but not overpowering Clam taste. One of our chefs, internationally trained Jack Jones, came up with just the taste that I wanted after a little bit of experimenting.

In the 1980s, Seattle hosted a massive Chowder Cook-Off and invited all of Seattle's seafood restaurants to compete. Duke's won by a landslide. I knew our Chowder was good, but this proved it was not just good—it was the best. After winning the competition for three consecutive years, the organizers invited me to retire and become a "celebrity" judge the following year. This successfully elevated Duke's Chowder to the Chowder against which all others would be measured. Winning this competition launched our company to a new level and started our journey down the successful road leading to our position as the leader in sourcing Sustainable Seafood. We had what every company looks for, a unique offering. Award Winning Chowder would serve our company well for the years to come.

Not long after I began tinkering with my grandfather's Chowder recipe, my mind was racing with all kinds of ideas and potential flavors. Could anything be better than Clam Chowder? I got into the kitchen with our chefs and opened up a whole new world of Chowder with over twenty-five new Chowder recipes. I'm not going to say any are my favorite because they are all spectacular. If anyone asks, you just say, "You have to try the Chowder at Duke's!"

# Key Tips from Chef "Wild" Bill for Duke's Clam Chowder:

- When the recipe calls for a roux, it is cooked for exactly 7 minutes after the Chowder reaches 175 degrees. This allows the flour to cook out and eliminates the gluey, pasty taste of most Chowders.

- We use heavy whipping cream (butterfat content of 39-41 percent) with no rBST (artificial growth hormones that are given to dairy cows to increase their milk production), which gives the Chowder a silky finish.

- The "herbiness" is from the combination of basil, dill, marjoram, parsley and thyme. These flavors are the perfect complement to the Clams.

- Our IQF (individually quick frozen) Clams are chemical-free, and our bacon contains no sodium nitrite. We obtain Clams harvested from off the coast of Martha's Vineyard. Most restaurants use canned Clams with tripolyphosphate and bacon with sodium nitrite.

- Notice there's no carrots in our recipe. Their sweetness adds the wrong accent. Stick with celery (for crunch) and red potatoes (for body).

- And now it is gluten-free, along with all our other Chowders.

## Storing Chowders:

- If serving the next day, after Chowder is finished simmering, place in a shallow pan (so that Chowder is no more than 2 inches thick) and refrigerate. This will allow the mixture to get below 41 degrees quickly in the proper time for safe food handling.

## Chowder Base:

- Custom Culinary makes an all-natural Clam base developed for Duke's under the Gold Label Clam brand. They also make all-natural Shrimp, Crab, Lobster, and chicken bases. They can be purchased in 1 lb containers on Amazon.com.

### Note from Duke:

Missing from our Chowders is the recipe for the "Un"Chowder, Chicken Noodle Soup. Introduced by Rik Kessler, former chef and good friend, this recipe is for another publication. We served it for years and many guests claim it cured them of sickness. It did the same for me when I was sick in bed with a temperature of 102° many years ago. Stay tuned.

# DUKE'S AWARD WINNING CLAM CHOWDER gf

This is the recipe that started it all . . . a revolutionary new spin on my grandfather's old recipe that has continued to bring people to Duke's since 1983. Unprecedented Winner of the Seattle Chowder Cook-Off three years in a row.

Makes ¾ gallon

## Ingredients

2 cups baby red potatoes, diced medium

4 slices nitrite-free bacon

½ cup Darigold butter

2 cups onions, diced medium

2 cups celery, diced medium

1 Tbsp fresh garlic, diced small

½ cup flour or Duke's Gluten-Free Flour Blend (pg 174)

2 Tbsp Clam base

1½ cups Clam juice

1½ cups milk

2½ cups heavy whipping cream

½ tsp fresh organic basil leaves, diced small

1 tsp fresh organic thyme, stems removed, diced small

½ tsp fresh marjoram, diced small

½ tsp black pepper

2 Tbsp fresh organic parsley, stems removed, diced small

1 Tbsp fresh organic dill, stems removed, diced small

1 lb IQF (individually quick frozen) Surf Clams (all natural)

## Directions

- Blanch potatoes in boiling water until tender. Drain and set aside.

- In a separate bowl, mix Clam base with Clam juice until dissolved.

- Chop bacon (diced medium), and cook in heavy-bottomed saucepan until crispy. Add butter, onions, celery and garlic, and sauté until tender.

- Then, add flour and stir well to incorporate. This is the roux. Continue stirring and bring mixture to 175 degrees. Then cook for exactly 7 minutes. Do not brown the roux.

- Add Clam base/Clam juice mixture to the roux. (Adding it after the roux has cooked prevents roux balls from forming.)

- Add the milk and cream, then the herbs. Heat until 185 degrees, blending constantly with a wire whisk.

- Add blanched red potatoes and Clams. Simmer at 185 degrees for 2 to 3 minutes. Turn heat down and hold at 165-175 degrees.

 Tip from Chef "Wild" Bill:

The Chowder will taste dramatically better when the herbs have bloomed and the flavors have fully developed after simmering for a few hours.

3-Time Seattle Chowder Cook-Off Winner

# BUTTERNUT PRAWN CHOWDER gf

This "sweet" and rich Chowder pulls from the unique combination of garlic, onions, celery, butter, basil, parsley and roasted red bell peppers, but the secret ingredient is a mild curry addition, which brings the flavor to a place you won't soon forget.

Makes ⅓ gallon

## Ingredients

1 cup organic baby red potatoes, diced medium

½ cup Darigold butter

¼ cup onions, diced medium

¼ cup celery, diced medium

1 tsp fresh garlic, diced small

½ cup flour or Duke's Gluten-Free Flour Blend (pg 174)

¼ cup all-natural Shrimp base

2 cups hot water

½ cup roasted red bell peppers, peeled, stemmed, de-seeded and puréed

1 tsp fresh organic basil, diced small

1 Tbsp fresh organic parsley, stems removed, diced small

1 tsp yellow curry powder

pinch sea salt

½ tsp black pepper

½ tsp Old Bay Seasoning

1 cup heavy whipping cream

½ pound (about 1 cup) Wild Mexican Prawns, thawed under running cold water, peeled and deveined

## Directions

- Broil the red peppers on the BBQ or roast in the oven until peppers are soft and the skins begin to blister. Place peppers in a large bowl and cover with plastic wrap for 10 minutes. Skins should fall right off. Set aside.

- Cook potatoes in salted boiling water until al dente. Run under cool water until chilled; then drain and set aside.

- In a separate bowl, mix Shrimp base and water, and stir until dissolved. This is the Shrimp stock.

- In a heavy-gauge soup pot, melt butter, and sauté onions, celery and garlic until soft.

- Then, add flour and stir well to incorporate. This is the roux. Continue stirring and bring mixture to 175 degrees; then cook for exactly 7 minutes. Do not brown the roux.

- Slowly add Shrimp stock to the roux and stir until evenly incorporated. Add puréed pepper, herbs, spices and cream, and bring to 180 degrees. Add cooked potatoes and maintain at 175 degrees while you prepare Prawns.

- To prepare Prawns, lightly dust them with a pinch of curry powder, sea salt, black pepper and parsley, and sauté in olive oil for 6 minutes or until they have lost all translucency. Reserve four Prawns to hang off the side of the cup or bowl for garnish. Dice remaining Prawns and add to Chowder and cook for 3 more minutes.

 Tip from Chef "Wild" Bill:

If serving the next day, before preparing and adding Prawns, place in a shallow pan (Chowder not more than 2 inches thick) and refrigerate. This will allow the mixture to get below 41 degrees quickly in the proper time for safe food handling. When ready to serve, re-heat to 165-175 degrees, and prepare and add Prawns as instructed above.

# NORTH BY NORTHWEST SEAFOOD CHOWDER gf

This Manhattan-style Chowder is a red Chowder that is distinguished by the presence of small chunky tomatoes. It also contains no dairy or gluten, making it a lighter Chowder for those times when cream and butter might seem a bit too heavy. You can pretty much use any seafood that is available.

Serves two

## Chowder Ingredients

4 oz Wild Alaska Salmon

4 oz Wild Alaska whitefish (Halibut, Cod or Rockfish)

1¼ cups North by Northwest Seafood Chowder Base

4 fresh Mussels (we use Penn Cove) de-bearded, or 4 fresh Manila Clams (Penn Cove for sure)

1 Tbsp fresh organic basil, diced small

## Directions

• Fillet seafood using the deep-skin method, which is to remove the gray matter along with the skin, and pluck the bones from whitefish and pin bones from Salmon with your fingers or with needle-nose pliers or boning tweezers if necessary. If you are buying from your local fishmonger, ask to have the fillet deep-skinned as well.

• Cut seafood in to small pieces, about ½ oz each.

• In a sauté pan, heat North by Northwest Seafood Chowder Base to 170 degrees and poach seafood until translucency is gone, approximately five minutes. Mussels should be fully open.

• Top with fresh organic basil.

 Tip from Chef "Wild" Bill:

For great-tasting cooked tomatoes, score each tomato and boil in lightly salted water. When the skins begin to separate, remove from heat and shock in ice water until chilled. Skins will slide right off.

## Seafood Chowder Base Ingredients

¼ cup extra virgin olive oil

¼ cup celery, diced medium

¼ cup carrots, peeled, diced medium

¼ cup sweet onions, diced medium

2 Tbsp fresh garlic cloves, diced small

2 cups cooked tomatoes, seeds removed, diced small (see tip below)

¼ cup tomato paste

1 Tbsp fresh organic oregano, stems removed, diced small

1 Tbsp fresh organic thyme, stems removed, diced small

¼ cup fresh organic basil leaves, thinly sliced

1 Tbsp black pepper

2 Tbsp fish base (chemical free, all natural)

1 cup water

## Directions

• Heat olive oil in a large saucepan, and then add celery, carrots, onions and garlic. Simmer on medium heat until all vegetables are soft but not browned. Add all remaining ingredients, stirring continuously, and simmer over medium heat for about 20 minutes.

# DUNGENESS CRABBY BABY BISQUE gf

Ohhh, Dungeness Crab . . . it is undeniably and heavenly delicious. This dish combines the rich, sweet and salty flavor of local Dungie Crab that will hit the spot.

Makes 1 gallon

## Ingredients

1 cup shallots

1 cup celery

½ cup unsalted Darigold butter

6 cups all-natural Clam juice

¼ cup Crab base

1 cup tomato paste

½ cup flour or Duke's Gluten-Free Flour Blend (pg 174)

1 Tbsp Old Bay seasoning

1½ tsp cayenne pepper

1 Tbsp paprika

1½ cup dry sherry

2½ cups heavy whipping cream

¼ lb (about ½ cup) Dungeness Crabmeat

## Directions

- Mix Clam juice, Crab base and tomato paste in a separate mixing bowl until incorporated.

- Purée shallots and celery in a food processor; then sauté them in butter until soft (do not brown) in a heavy-gauge soup pot.

- Add flour and stir well to incorporate. This is the roux. Continue stirring and bring mixture to 175 degrees; then cook for exactly 7 minutes. Do not brown the roux.

- While stirring, slowly add Clam/Crab/tomato paste mixture to the roux. Add spices, sherry and cream, and bring to 185 degrees.

- Add Crab and cook for 2 minutes. Serve at 175 degrees. Garnish with Crab claw (optional).

- For added Crab flavor, sprinkle additional Crabmeat on top.

# DUNGENESS CRAB & BOURBON CHOWDER gf

This crazy concoction combines with the sweet caramel notes in the bourbon and all the fresh ingredients to make a Chowder unlike any I've ever had.

Makes ½ gallon

## Ingredients

- 1 cup organic baby red potatoes, diced
- ½ cup Darigold butter
- ½ cup sweet onions, diced medium
- ½ cup celery, diced medium
- ½ cup flour or Duke's Gluten-Free Flour Blend (pg 174)
- 2 Tbsp all-natural Crab base
- ½ cup hot water
- ¼ cup Jack Daniel's or Duke's Blend Woodford Reserve Bourbon
- 2 cups heavy whipping cream
- ½ cup fresh sweet corn
- ½ tsp fresh organic thyme, stems removed, diced small
- ½ tsp fresh organic tarragon, stems removed, diced small
- ½ tsp black pepper
- 1 tsp Old Bay Seasoning
- ½ lb (about 1 cup) fresh Washington, Oregon or Alaska Dungeness Crabmeat
- ½ tsp fresh organic parsley, stems removed, diced small

## Directions

- Boil chopped baby reds in lightly salted water until al dente. Drain and cool and set aside.
- In a separate bowl, mix Crab base and hot water until dissolved. This is the stock.
- In a heavy-gauge soup pot, melt butter. Add onions and celery, and sauté until veggies are soft.
- Then, add flour and stir well to incorporate. This is the roux. Continue stirring and bring mixture to 175 degrees and cook for exactly 7 minutes. Do not brown.
- Slowly add stock to the roux and stir until smooth.
- Add whiskey and stir until smooth.
- Add cream, corn, cooked potatoes, thyme, tarragon and spices and bring to 180 degrees for 3 minutes.
- Serve Chowder at 175 degrees. Top with Dungeness Crabmeat, a small pinch of Old Bay Seasoning and chopped parsley.

 Tips from Chef "Wild" Bill:

- Roasting fresh whole corn cobs on the broiler, then carving the kernels off the cob gives this Chowder extra color and a slightly smoky flavor profile.

- If serving the next day, before adding Crab, seasoning and parsley, place in a shallow pan (Chowder not more than 2 inches thick) and refrigerate. This will allow the mixture to get below 41 degrees quickly in the proper time for safe food handling. When ready to serve, reheat to 165-175 degrees and add garnishes and Crab as instructed above.

# LOBSTER MOBSTER PERNOD CHOWDER gf

Pernod, an alcoholic liqueur relative to the Greek liqueur ouzo, brings a delightful hint of black licorice flavor to this Duke's favorite. Don't be afraid of the licorice, though. It produces a unique blend that creates its very own flavor, barely detectable. Langostinos (not truly Lobster, but known as such because of their Lobster-like taste and shape), combined together with a Lobster base, make this Chowder a truly unique dish you will only find at Duke's.

Makes 1 gallon

## Ingredients

2 cups sweet potatoes, peeled and diced into 1" cubes

5 cups hot water

½ cup all-natural Lobster base

2 cups Darigold butter

1 cup fennel, bulb only, diced medium

1 cup onions, diced medium

1 cup celery, diced medium

½ cup shallots, diced small

2 cups flour or Duke's Gluten-Free Flour Blend (pg 174)

3 cups heavy whipping cream

1 Tbsp black pepper

1 Tbsp fresh organic thyme, stems removed, diced small

2¼ tsp paprika

1 Tbsp fresh organic parsley, stems removed, diced small

2 cups cooked Langostinos

½ cup Pernod (Anisette or Sambuca will also work)

## Directions

- Boil sweet potatoes in lightly salted water until al dente. Drain and set aside.

- Mix hot water and Lobster base in a bowl, and stir until base is completely dissolved. This is the stock.

- In a heavy-gauge soup pot, melt butter. Add fennel, onion, celery and shallots and sauté over medium heat until soft.

- Then, add flour and stir well to incorporate. This is the roux. Continue stirring and bring mixture to 175 degrees; then cook for exactly 7 minutes. Do not brown the roux.

- With a wire whisk, slowly add stock to roux mixture (adding it after the roux has cooked prevents roux balls from forming).

- Whisking constantly, bring mixture to 180 degrees. Add cream and spices and return mixture to 180 degrees.

- Add Langostinos and Pernod, and heat to 190 degrees for 5 minutes. Turn heat down and hold at 165-175 degrees.

 Tip from Chef "Wild" Bill:

The Chowder will taste dramatically better when the herbs have bloomed and the flavors have fully developed after simmering for a few hours.

# RAGIN' CAJUN CHICKEN CORN CHOWDER gf

This spicy Chowder was approved by a bona-fide Cajun. It's a bit spicy, but not enough to take your head off. Just to be safe, you may want to have a napkin nearby to wipe your brow.

Makes 1 gallon

## Ingredients

1 cup baby red potatoes, diced medium

1 cup Darigold butter

4 Tbsp Blackening Spice Of Life (pg 323)

1 cup sweet onions, diced medium

1 cup celery, diced medium

1 Tbsp fresh garlic, diced small

1 cup flour or Duke's Gluten-Free Flour Blend (pg 174)

¼ cup all-natural chicken base

4 cups hot water

1 cup sweet corn kernels (fresh if possible)

1½ tsp black pepper

½ Tbsp cumin

1 Tbsp fresh organic parsley, stems removed, diced small

¼ cup fresh organic cilantro, stems removed, diced small

6 cups heavy whipping cream

dollop (2 Tbsp) sour cream

green, yellow and red peppers, julienne-sliced

2 cups organic chicken breast, diced medium

## Directions

- Boil chopped baby reds in lightly salted water until al dente. Drain and set aside.

- In a separate bowl, stir chicken base into hot water until dissolved.

- In heavy-gauge soup pot, melt butter. Evenly coat cubed chicken with Blackening Spice Of Life and sauté until done. Remove from pan and set aside. Add onions, celery and garlic to soup pot and cook for 1-2 minutes.

- Then, add flour and stir well to incorporate. This is the roux. Continue stirring and bring mixture to 175 degrees; then cook for exactly 7 minutes. Do not brown the roux.

- Slowly add chicken base/water mixture into the roux, stirring continuously to incorporate.

- Add cooked chicken, cooked potatoes, corn, spices, herbs and whipping cream and bring to 180 degrees for 5 minutes. Serve at 175 degrees. Garnish with a dollop of sour cream.

 Tip from Chef "Wild" Bill:

If broiling corn on the cob, save some for a garnish. It's unbelievably tasty. Also, if you like a little more spice, add more blackening seasoning.

# HENRI PUJO'S CRAYFISH CHOWDER gf

The late Henri Pujo-Perissere, French chef, inventor and friend, cooked this for me in our first Duke's on lower Queen Anne in the late 1980s. Sherry is the magic ingredient; it pulls all the flavors together into a sensual stew better than any aphrodisiac.

Makes 1 gallon

## Ingredients

1 cup sweet potatoes, peeled, diced medium

1 cup Darigold butter

½ cup sweet onions, diced medium

½ cup celery, diced medium

½ cup carrots, peeled, diced medium

1 cup flour or Duke's Gluten-Free Flour Blend (pg 174)

8 cups Crayfish stock (pg 172)

3 Tbsp Durkees Red Hot Sauce

1 cup heavy whipping cream

½ cup dry sherry

1 lb Crayfish tail meat, diced medium

## Directions

• Boil sweet potatoes in lightly salted water until they begin to soften. Transfer potatoes to a colander and run under cold water. Set aside to drain.

• In a heavy-gauge soup pot, melt butter, and sauté onions, celery and carrots until soft.

• Then, add flour, and stir well to incorporate. This is the roux. Continue stirring and bring mixture to 175 degrees; then cook for exactly 7 minutes. Do not brown the roux.

• Stir in Crayfish stock and heat to 180 degrees. Add Crayfish, cooked potatoes, hot sauce, whipping cream and sherry, and bring back to 180 degrees. Serve at 165-180 degrees.

# CRAYFISH STOCK gf

## Ingredients

1 Tbsp extra virgin olive oil

¼ cup Walla Walla Sweet onions, diced medium

¼ cup carrots, peeled, diced medium

¼ cup fresh garlic, diced small

12 cups water

¼ lb whole Crayfish, crushed with a meat mallet into medium pieces

1 Tbsp fresh organic thyme, stems removed, diced small

¼ tsp Lea & Perrins Worcestershire Sauce

½ tsp cayenne pepper

¼ tsp white pepper

¼ tsp black pepper

¼ cup tomato paste

¼ cup Lobster base

¼ cup Shrimp base

½ tsp Tabasco sauce

## Directions

• In a heavy-gauge stockpot, heat olive oil on medium-high. Sauté onions, carrots and garlic until soft.

• Add water and remaining ingredients (including Crayfish shells) and bring to 195 degrees.

• Reduce heat and simmer on low for 3 hours.

• Strain using a fine-gauge strainer; there should be no shell pieces or veggies remaining. Makes about 8 cups of stock. Add water to bring it to 8 cups if necessary.

DukeWorthy™ Provider

## Blue Checked Everywhere

When Duke's opened in 1977, there were blue-checked napkins and tablecloths everywhere. It was a big part of our brand. When Service Linen Supply took over the linen account in the early '80s, Bob Raphael assured me that his "service" would be exceptional. He never let us down. The Raphael/Jassny families have gone the extra mile to provide us with "service" just like their company name. If we ran out of linen, Bob would drive it to us personally. If we needed help with a charity event, he was always right there. I think they ought to change their name to Exceptional Service Linen Supply.

# "Duke Was Born With An Amazing Palette"

We started working with Cuizina back in 2003 in order to make our Chowders more consistent. There are only two people who make our Chowder at Cuizina. In the past, we had fifteen people making it in our restaurants. This led to inconsistency. Cuizina uses our recipe, our specific ingredients from our suppliers, and it does it well. The staff is great to work with and is always receptive to any improvements we want to institute.

Here's what Pat Flin, head chef of Cuizina, said about working with Duke, "Duke was born with an amazing palette—you can't hide anything from him!"

Ben Piatt of Cuizina said, "Duke always wants the best ingredients, which is a perfect match for our operation. Quality matters to Duke, and it does to us as well. We take pride in using fresh ingredients, practicing the highest industry safety standards, and creating delicious recipes. Working with Duke is a collaborative effort. He is very hands-on and informed about what he's doing and cooking. At one time, Cuizina was manufacturing twelve different Chowder recipes that were Duke's creations."

Pat continued, "Beyond that, he's fun to work with. During demos at Costco, Duke would don a rain slicker and Sou'wester to run around and serve samples to Costco members. It always created quite a buzz around the demo station and gave members a good sense of the enjoyment that Duke has in creating his Chowders (not to mention that they are delicious)."

# DUKE'S GLUTEN-FREE FLOUR BLEND gf

Many years ago, my daughter Amy was diagnosed with gluten intolerance. This, of course, meant no more Duke's Chowder, and that just could not be. So I started investigating how we could make our Chowder gluten-free. This was a challenging task since there weren't enough resources early on even to come close. But we kept trying as the gluten-free trend continued to grow, in part by people with true gluten intolerance, but also in part by people refusing to tolerate gluten. Finally, I met Denise Cooley, an expert on blending gluten-free flours. She created the perfect gluten-free flour blend for our Chowders. After much concern about people not liking this change, I can honestly say that not one person has mentioned any difference with Duke's Gluten-Free Flour Blend. Truth be told, you can't even tell the difference. Now my daughter and anyone refusing to tolerate gluten can eat our Chowder. This blend can be substituted 1:1 for regular flour to make the roux.

## Ingredients

1 cup tapioca starch

2½ cups white rice flour

4 cups potato starch

4½ cups sweet white sorghum flour

7 cups brown rice flour

## Directions

• Combine and keep in an airtight container.

## Duke Is A Clamologist

**DukeWorthy™ Provider**

When I visited the Surf Clam operations of Sea Watch back in Maryland many years ago, I earned my degree of Certified "Clamologist" after taking the Clams 101 course. I was fascinated with the capture and processing of the Clams that wind up in our Chowder. The Clams are big, much bigger than West Coast Clams. They are also tender and have a wonderful Clam perfume that is truly unique. No other creature smells like these bivalves. Their operation is also environmentally friendly. The ocean floor is better off because of their participation.

Sea Watch has been supplying the Clams for Duke's Award Winning Clam Chowder since Duke's started producing the Chowder in the early 1980s. The sea Clams that go into every bowl of Duke's Award Winning Clam Chowder are Wild harvested off of the East Coast near Martha's Vineyard in an environmentally friendly manner by Sea Watch's very own boats. They are then frozen without any chemicals or preservatives to ensure the freshest quality for each bowl of Chowder.

**SEAWATCH®**
**INTERNATIONAL**

WAITER SPIKE RECOMMENDS FRESH CLAM CHOWDER BEFORE KITCHEN RUNS OUT.

Meet Seattle's most famous Duke, Duke Moscrip.

When he opened his first restaurant over 20 years ago, he introduced a clam chowder recipe inspired by his grandfather. Today, you can enjoy Duke's award-winning clam chowder and seven other chowders as well, from smoked salmon to crab.

"After my Grandfather gave me his clam chowder recipe, I began thinking about other chowders," Duke explains. "Could anything be better than clam chowder? So I started experimenting with crab, lobster, mussels, crayfish and some of my other favorite foods. Boy did I have fun tasting with all my chefs!"

And you'll have fun, too. Because along with the chowders, you'll find a lot of great seafood dishes, salads, and sandwiches, including Duke's classic cheeseburger.

Yes, a cheeseburger at a Chowder House, because, as Duke says, "everybody's gotta have a great cheeseburger."

Now there are four Duke's Chowder House locations. Each one is a comfortable and affordable neighborhood place, because Duke wanted to make sure you'd feel as relaxed in his restaurants as you do in your own kitchen.

Eat. Drink. Relax.

# The Duke of Chowder

# Succulent Wild Alaska Salmon

"If I had one thing to eat in this world, it would be Wild Alaska Salmon."

# On To Alaska For Wild Alaska Salmon

If I could choose only one thing to eat in this world, it would be Salmon. Its amazing, natural flavor is proof positive that healthy food can taste good. I am so hooked on Salmon that I eat it for breakfast about five days per week. I swear that I feel invigorated with every flavorful bite of this extremely nutrient-dense healthy food. With plenty of Omega-3 fatty acids, it will keep your ticker strong and your mind sharp. As you've heard throughout this book, I am passionate about Wild Salmon and make sure that Duke's is always at the top of its game by checking in with our fish at the source. I travel to Alaska several times a year to spend time on the water with the beloved fishermen who bring us this amazing fish. A special thanks to our many dedicated fisherwomen and fishermen all over Alaska who have made Duke's the premier seafood restaurant it has become.

## Ice-Chilled Better Than Fresh

In Copper River, the fishermen I work with ice their fish right at capture. Within 24-48 hours, they bring their catch to a large ship called a tender for processing. The fishermen empty their boat and are right back fishing while the tender gently transfers the fish in 33 degree seawater to Trident Seafoods in Cordova, Alaska. Trident is exceptional. It has consistent temperature control, rapid processing, thoughtful packaging and quick freezing. Freezing the fish quickly after the catch locks in freshness, ensuring that we get the most delicious-tasting Salmon on the planet.

In Yakutat, Southeast Alaska, we work with a gillnet fishery that produces incredible-tasting fish. All good Salmon fisheries ice the fish from the time they are caught to the time they are transferred to the processor. Yakutat Seafoods (partially owned and operated by Greg Indreland) keeps its fish iced throughout the processing. The fish are then flown to professionals at Pacific Seafood in Seattle, where they are filleted, vacuum packed and frozen.

I often say that "Fresh isn't fresh." All too often, "fresh" Salmon can be as old as twenty-five days! Many Alaska fishermen only buy "frozen at the source" Salmon because they know that the only way to lock in the Salmon's fresh, wild ocean flavor is rapid processing and freezing. This must be done because it is impossible to consistently control the two biggest enemies to great-tasting fish: time and temperature. Transporting the fish after capture can take many days, with bad weather postponing a ship's trip ashore. Fish that isn't frozen immediately could sit on a runway for days because that load of cargo was bumped by airlines. You may think Alaska is cold enough to keep fish chilled, but not during Salmon season. On a summer day, a black tarmac at the airport can get as hot as 90 degrees. In addition, Alaska has twenty hours of daylight during this time of year. Frozen fish experience none of these variables, and the clean, fresh taste is proof.

# "The Highest Quality That Is Truly Unparalleled"

**DukeWorthy™ Provider**

Larry Andrews, Retail Marketing Director of Alaska Seafood Marketing Institute, said, "Duke's is a great supporter of the Alaska seafood industry, purchasing thousands of pounds of Coho Salmon, Cod, Halibut, Scallops, and Rockfish as well as other products that are artfully prepared by Chef "Wild" Bill and his team. Duke has demonstrated a level of commitment to quality and the understanding of how the Alaska seafood industry works, from harvesting and processing to responsible fisheries management that is truly unparalleled. Duke's approach to seafood is something that is rarely seen in today's fast-paced world.

Duke has traveled extensively in Alaska and spent untold hours on the fishing grounds working directly with fishermen and processors to improve and build on sound handling techniques to ensure his restaurants deliver the highest quality seafood possible. As Duke says, his job is 'to learn how correct handling impacts the way that seafood tastes.' He takes an approach that ensures that the Alaska seafood he serves at all of his Chowder Houses is handled in a superior manner from catch to plate."

The Alaska Seafood Marketing Institute, ASMI, is a public-private partnership between the State of Alaska and the Alaska seafood industry, established to foster economic development of a renewable natural resource. ASMI is playing a key role in the repositioning of Alaska's seafood industry as a competitive market-driven food production industry. Its work to boost the value of Alaska's seafood product portfolio is accomplished through partnerships with retail grocers, foodservice distributors, restaurant chains like ours, foodservice operators, universities, culinary schools, and the media.

Alaska Seafood Marketing Institute has been very influential in our developing knowledge of the different seafood species, the Alaska fishing grounds, the fishermen and fisherwomen in Alaska and the processing plants all over Alaska. My good friend Larry Andrews has helped guide me in my efforts to learn about the resources in Alaska. We wouldn't be as far along in our understanding of the world of seafood without his help.

**ALASKA SEAFOOD**

*Wild, Natural & Sustainable*®

# WILD ALASKA SALMON CHERRIES EVERYWHERE gf

Another play on the salty sweetness we all inherently crave. This recipe is best during cherry season when cherries are everywhere—local, fresh, abundant and worth waiting for.

Serves three

## Ingredients

Three 8 oz Wild Alaska Salmon fillets

1½ tsp extra virgin olive oil

15 cherries, stems and pits removed and cut in half

1 tsp fresh organic basil leaves, minced

6 Tbsp Grand Marnier

9 Tbsp chilled Darigold butter

## Directions

- Fillet Salmon using the deep-skin method, which is to remove the gray matter along with the skin and pluck the pin bones with needle-nose pliers or boning tweezers. If you are buying from your local fishmonger, ask to have the fillet deep-skinned as well.

- In a sauté pan, heat olive oil on high but do not smoke.

- Pan-sear Salmon on one side for 3-4 minutes, flip, add cherries and cook for about 3-4 minutes or until fish has lost all its translucency (cherries should be slightly soft). Add fresh organic basil, then deglaze with Grand Marnier (Deglazing, Demystified, pg 326).

- Remove from heat (sauce will separate if it gets too hot) and swirl in butter.

- Serve cherries on top of Salmon with extra sauce in a small bowl.

# CRABBY PEPPERED WILD ALASKA SALMON gf

This dish was inspired by my love for peppered steak. Fresh ground pepper covering a beautiful fillet of Salmon combines with a Duke's twist . . . bleu cheese dressing.

Serves two

## Ingredients

Two 8 oz Wild Alaska Salmon fillets

½ cup Nothing But Blue Sky Bleu Cheese Dressing (pg 139)

2 tsp freshly ground black pepper

½ cup fresh Dungeness Crabmeat

## Directions

• Fillet Salmon using the deep-skin method, which is to remove the gray matter along with the skin and pluck the pin bones with needle-nose pliers or boning tweezers. If you are buying from your local fishmonger, ask to have the fillet deep-skinned as well.

• Press black pepper into the top of the Salmon fillets.

• Broil Salmon for 3-4 minutes per side or until fish has lost all its translucency.

• Create a puddle of Nothing But Blue Sky Bleu Cheese Dressing on a plate and place Salmon in puddle. Top with Dungeness Crab and decorate with a Maris leg (the puffiest part of the largest leg) section.

 Tip from Chef "Wild" Bill:

Our Nothing But Blue Sky Bleu Cheese Dressing is also gluten-free because the Roth brand "Buttermilk Blue" is not grown on bread like most other bleu cheese.

# Silky Sensual Pan Seared Wild Alaska Salmon gf

This recipe was inspired from a magazine photo I fell in love with years ago. Chef "Wild" Bill played around with the idea and the results were an instant hit, making this one of Duke's most popular dishes.

Serves two

## Ingredients

Two 8 oz Wild Alaska Salmon fillets

2 tsp extra virgin olive oil

2 tsp fresh organic ginger, minced

2 tsp fresh organic basil leaves, stems removed, diced small

2 Tbsp granulated sugar mixed with a pinch of fresh cracked black pepper

½ cup white wine

½ cup Fill Me Up Buttercup Butta Cream Sauce (pg 149)

1 tsp Balsamic Soy Reduction Sauce (pg 322)

## Directions

- Fillet Salmon using the deep-skin method, which is to remove the gray matter along with the skin and pluck the pin bones with needle-nose pliers or boning tweezers. If you are buying from your local fishmonger, ask to have the fillet deep-skinned as well.

- Mix a small amount of olive oil with the ginger. (This will slow the browning process.) Then rub on Salmon. Press basil into Salmon and refrigerate for at least 2 hours.

- Preheat oven to 425.

- On a stovetop burner, heat a sauté pan and add olive oil until hot but not smoking. Press sugar/pepper mixture into the top of the Salmon. Sauté Salmon carefully—only caramelize the sugar; do not carbonize or char. Salmon should have a deep "caramel" color. Flip Salmon.

- Deglaze with white wine (Deglazing, Demystified, pg 326).

- Bake Salmon for 5 minutes or until fish has lost all its translucency.

- On your serving plate, create a puddle of the Fill Me Up Buttercup Butta Cream Sauce (it should take up about ½ the plate) and add cooked Salmon. Ladle the Balsamic Soy Reduction Sauce over the Salmon until it runs onto the Fill Me Up Buttercup Butta Cream Sauce. Drag a toothpick through the sauces to decorate.

# OH SO BLUEBERRY & GOAT CHEESE WILD ALASKA SALMON gf

Apparently, some people only dream in black and white. I suppose I am lucky since I often dream of colorful, delicious food. Maybe it's because I've been completely immersed in it most of my life. One such dream is how this recipe came to life. I woke up with the idea of combining blueberries and goat cheese together, but I pondered, "What could we serve it with?" The idea zapped me like a lightning bolt—Wild Alaska Salmon, of course. Turns out, it's incredible.

The blueberries we use are from Oregon; ironically, they are the Duke variety, picked at the peak of sweetness, then preserved with just enough sugar to match the brix in the berry. This avoids the over-sweetened taste of most blueberry preserves.

Rik Kessler, former Chef and good friend, introduced us to the best goat cheese in the world. The goat cheese comes from a high-quality producer named Laura Chenel from Carneros, California. The early morning fog is still lingering on the meadows of the farms when the milk is received and quality parameters are checked. Only the best goat milk is used, and you can really taste the difference. Her goat cheese is unbelievably delicious.

Serves two

## Ingredients

Two 8 oz Wild Alaska Salmon fillets

½ cup goat cheese (we use Laura Chenel brand), shaped into two rounds

40 blueberries

2 Tbsp fresh organic basil leaves, stems removed, diced small

4 Tbsp orange liqueur (Grand Marnier or Cointreau)

## Directions

• Fillet Salmon using the deep-skin method, which is to remove the gray matter along with the skin and pluck the pin bones with needle-nose pliers or boning tweezers. If you are buying from your local fishmonger, ask to have the fillet deep-skinned as well.

• Broil Salmon for 3-4 minutes per side or until fish has lost all its translucency.

• Top with goat cheese and place under broiler or cheese melter until goat cheese melts—don't take your eye off of it—this should take approximately 2 minutes, but every broiler is different. Remove from broiler.

• In a small sauté pan, "bloom" the blueberries by cooking them with the orange liquer and basil on medium-high heat for 1 minute. (Do not overcook.)

• Spoon the blueberry/basil mixture over goat cheese and Salmon. Then pour remaining liquid into a small ramekin for dipping.

# WILD ALASKA SALMON FORTUNATO gf

Chef "Wild" Bill and I were fortunate to work with celebrated local Chef Monique Barbeau, who was a star chef back in the days before chefs became "celebrities." She inspired the idea for this recipe. When you taste this delicious blend of Mediterranean-style flavors, the "fortunato" will be all yours. Also, try this recipe with Halibut (see Forget Me Not)

Serves two

## Ingredients

Two 8 oz Wild Alaska Salmon fillets

½ cup Sundried Tomato Relish (pg 329)

24 pine nuts

## Directions

- Fillet Salmon using the deep-skin method, which is to remove the gray matter along with the skin and pluck the pin bones with needle-nose pliers or boning tweezers. If you are buying from your local fishmonger, ask to have the fillet deep-skinned as well.

- Broil Salmon forfor 3-4 minutes per side or until fish has lost all its translucency. To check the middle for doneness, place a spatula under fish about halfway; lift up until the fillet breaks open. It's okay to have a small crack in the surface of your fish; better to have the correct doneness than a pretty fillet that is raw or overdone. The trick to Salmon is not to overcook because it can get very dry.

- Transfer to a plate and top with Sundried Tomato Relish.

- Sprinkle with pine nuts.

# WILD ALASKA SALMON WITH PRETTY PESTO gf

We call it "pretty" pesto because Chef "Wild" Bill's pesto is an incredible bright green and can really only be described as, well . . . pretty. The pesto itself tastes "pretty" delicious, too!

Serves two

## Ingredients

Two 8 oz Wild Alaska Salmon fillets

large pinch Duke's Ready Anytime Seasoning (pg 323)

½ cup Basil Almond Pretty Pesto (pg 320)

## Directions

- Fillet Salmon using the deep-skin method, which is to remove the gray matter along with the skin and pluck the pin bones with needle-nose pliers or boning tweezers. If you are buying from your local fishmonger, ask to have the fillet deep-skinned as well.

- Sprinkle Salmon with Duke's Ready Anytime Seasoning and broil for for 3-4 minutes per side or until fish has lost all its translucency.

- Top with Basil Almond Pretty Pesto.

# WILD ALASKA SALMON "OSCAR WILDE" gf

Steak Oscar is great, but with Wild Salmon, it's a knockout.

Serves two

## Ingredients

Two 8 oz Wild Alaska Salmon fillets

large pinch Duke's Ready Anytime Seasoning (pg 323)

14 medium fresh asparagus spears

½ cup Dungeness Crabmeat

½ cup "Holidays" Hollandaise Sauce (pg 146)

## Directions

- Fillet Salmon using the deep-skin method, which is to remove the gray matter along with the skin and pluck the pin bones with needle-nose pliers or boning tweezers. If you are buying from your local fishmonger, ask to have the fillet deep-skinned as well.

- Warm "Holidays" Hollandaise Sauce, but keep it from getting too hot.

- Sprinkle Duke's Ready Anytime Seasoning on Salmon. Rub your BBQ grates with vegetable oil (this keeps the fish from sticking) and broil Salmon.

- When Salmon is halfway done (about 3-4 minutes), flip and separately add asparagus spears to the grill.

- Turn asparagus several times on the grill until hot, but al dente, while Salmon finishes cooking (about 3-4 minutes).

- Serve Salmon topped with asparagus, Crab and "Holidays" Hollandaise Sauce.

# DUKE'S FAVORITE PASTA WITH WILD ALASKA SALMON

I know that I never say I have a favorite dish at Duke's other than anything Salmon. So, maybe this is a perfect blend of "I never say . . . " and "I guess I did." One of our chefs fixed this for me over twenty years ago, and I fell in love with it immediately. I'm a sucker for garlic cream sauce, and the peppers provide a perfect zing. It truly is my favorite pasta dish.

Serves one

## Ingredients

8 oz Wild Alaska Salmon fillet

½ lb gemelli pasta (we use Barilla brand)

1 Tbsp Blackening Spice Of Life (pg 323)

1 Tbsp Let's Be Clarified Butter (pg 148)

1 Tbsp fresh garlic, diced small

1¼ cup heavy whipping cream

1 Tbsp Duke's Superb Herb Blend (pg 322)

large pinch Duke's Ready Anytime Seasoning (pg 323)

1 tsp fresh organic basil leaves, stems removed, diced small

2 Tbsp Garlic Lover's Butter (pg 148)

2 Tbsp Parmesan cheese and 2 Tbsp Asiago cheese, grated and mixed together

¼ cup red, yellow and green peppers, julienne-sliced and caramelized

¼ cup Walla Walla Sweet onions, julienne-sliced and caramelized

pinch fresh organic parsley

## Directions

- Fillet Salmon using the deep-skin method, which is to remove the gray matter along with the skin and pluck the pin bones with needle-nose pliers or boning tweezers. If you are buying from your local fishmonger, ask to have the fillet deep-skinned as well.

- Cook pasta in four quarts of boiling salted water for 10 minutes.

- In sauté pan, caramelize peppers and onions.

- Drain pasta using a colander and set aside.

- At the same time, coat Salmon on one side only with Blackening Spice Of Life and caramelize seasoning side down in sauté pan in Let's Be Clarified Butter (spices should be melted) for 3-4 minutes. Flip Salmon and cook for 3-4 minutes or until fish has lost all its translucency.

- In a sauté pan, heat garlic, heavy whipping cream, Duke's Superb Herb Blend, Duke's Ready Anytime Seasoning and basil. Reduce until thickened, about 3 minutes.

- Stir in Garlic Lover's Butter until incorporated. Add cooked pasta and half of the cheese.

- Pour into a large bowl and garnish with remaining cheese and parsley.

- Top with sizzling-hot blackened Salmon, caramelized peppers and onions. Garnish with parsley.

 Tip from Chef "Wild" Bill:

Don't blacken both sides of the fish unless you really like it spicy hot. This can also overwhelm the Salmon's wonderful fragrance.

# OFF THE HOOK STUFFED WILD ALASKA SALMON

Literally and figuratively, this Salmon is "Off the Hook!" Crab and Salmon dance a delicious duet in this wonderful recipe.

Serves one

## Ingredients

8 oz Wild Alaska Salmon fillet

6 Tbsp It's Sooo Good Seafood Stuffing (pg 329)

1 Tbsp breadcrumbs

¼ cup Fill Me Up Buttercup Butta Cream Sauce (pg 149)

2 Tbsp Incredibly Healthy Vegetable Stock (pg 326)

## Directions

• Fillet Salmon using the deep-skin method, which is to remove the gray matter along with the skin and pluck the pin bones with needle-nose pliers or boning tweezers. If you are buying from your local fishmonger, ask to have the fillet deep-skinned as well.

• Preheat oven to 425 degrees.

• Cut a "pocket" into fillet. Lay the Salmon on a cutting board. Without cutting through the fillet, start from the top corner and cut diagonally on the bias into the fish 2½ inches deep.

• Place Salmon in a baking pan. Add stuffing to the pocket. (Some of the stuffing will be showing outside the fillet.)

• Sprinkle breadcrumbs over the exposed stuffing, which will turn crisp and golden brown when cooked.

• Slowly add vegetable stock to the baking pan, being careful not to get the breadcrumbs wet. Bake stuffed Salmon for 8 minutes or until fish has lost all its translucency (cooking times vary depending on thickness).

# MEDITERRANEAN HEIRLOOM TOMATO WILD ALASKA SALMON gf

Celebrated local Chef Monique Barbeau also inspired this recipe, and the unique combination of flavors will impress any foodie. It looks beautiful on the plate, too.

Serves one

## Ingredients

8 oz Wild Alaska Salmon fillet

6 Tbsp Feta cheese

¼ cup Duke's North by Northwest Seafood Chowder Base (pg 160)

large pinch Duke's Ready Anytime Seasoning (pg 323)

2 heirloom tomatoes, sliced thin and fanned out on a plate

½ cup Heirloom Tomato Salsa (see below)

## Directions

- Fillet Salmon using the deep-skin method, which is to remove the gray matter along with the skin and pluck the pin bones with needle-nose pliers or boning tweezers. If you are buying from your local fishmonger, ask to have the fillet deep-skinned as well.

- Sprinkle Duke's Ready Anytime Seasoning on Salmon. Rub your BBQ grates with vegetable oil (this keeps the fish from sticking) and broil Salmon for 3-4 minutes per side or until fish has lost all its translucency.

- Heat Duke's North by Northwest Seafood Chowder Base in pan to 175 degrees. Pour into large shallow bowl.

- Sprinkle with Feta cheese.

- Place Salmon on Feta and Seafood Chowder Base.

- Top with Heirloom Tomato Salsa.

# HEIRLOOM TOMATO SALSA gf

Some people call heirloom tomatoes ugly but Chef "Wild" Bill and I think they have a certain charm. It's best to make this salsa about an hour before serving so the flavors can get acquainted.

## Ingredients

2 cups heirloom tomatoes, diced medium

½ cup fresh organic basil leaves, sliced

1 tsp Duke's Ready Anytime Seasoning (pg 323)

¼ cup extra virgin olive oil

2 Tbsp balsamic vinegar

## Directions

- In a bowl, mix together.

# PUT YOUR HEAD ON MY PILLOW
# WILD ALASKA SALMON RAVIOLI

A little Northwest nod to Italy, these raviolis are as soft as a down pillow and stuffed with melt-in-your-mouth mascarpone cheese and delicious pumpkin.

Serves one

## Ingredients

8 oz Wild Alaska Salmon fillet, cut into 3 portions

9 fresh raviolis (use your favorite stuffing– Duke's uses pumpkin and mascarpone stuffed)

2 Tbsp Let's Be Clarified Butter (pg 148)

¼ cup squash or seasonal fresh vegetables

¾ cup heavy whipping cream

2 Tbsp Basil Almond Pretty Pesto (pg 320)

1 Tbsp Dukes' Superb Herb Blend (pg 322)

½ tsp Blackening Spice Of Life (pg 323)

1 Tbsp Parmesan cheese and 1 Tbsp Asiago cheese, grated fine and mixed together

2 Tbsp Garlic Lover's Butter (pg 148)

20 toasted pine nuts

## Directions

- Fillet Salmon using the deep-skin method, which is to remove the gray matter along with the skin and pluck the pin bones with needle-nose pliers or boning tweezers. If you are buying from your local fishmonger, ask him to fillet and deep-skin as well.

- Blanch raviolis in salted boiling water until they float to the top, about 5 minutes (7 minutes if frozen). Drain raviolis using a colander and set aside.

- Toss raviolis in a small amount of olive oil to prevent them from sticking together.

- In a saucepan, combine cream, Basil Almond Pretty Pesto and Duke's Superb Herb Blend and reduce over medium heat for 3-4 minutes.

- At the same time, add Blackening Spice Of Life to Salmon, and cook on a hot flat griddle or sauté pan in Let's Be Clarified Butter for 3-4 minutes per side or until fish has lost all its translucency.

- When the cream/pesto mixture begins to thicken, make the Alfredo sauce by stirring in ½ of the cheese and the Garlic Lover's Butter. Cook for approximately 3 more minutes or until Alfredo sauce has the consistency of applesauce—not runny or thick.

- Add ravioli to Alfredo sauce; then spoon onto a plate.

- Top with hot, blackened Salmon and garnish with remaining cheese and pine nuts.

# "WALK THE PLANK" WILD ALASKA SALMON gf

This dish is to "die for," but you won't literally have to walk the plank.

Serves two

## Ingredients

Two 8 oz Wild Alaska Salmon fillets

3 Tbsp Sinful Citrus Vinaigrette (pg 138)

2 Tbsp olive oil

2 Tbsp brown sugar

2 Tbsp Duke's Ready Anytime Seasoning (pg 323)

2 Tbsp Duke's Superb Herb Blend (pg 322)

1 cedar plank shingle cut in ½ lengthwise

 Tip from Chef "Wild" Bill:

When buying Salmon at the market, give the fish a good sniff. Fish should never smell "fishy" or be slimy. If you walk into a store or market and it smells "fishy," get your Salmon elsewhere. If Salmon isn't great, the best sauces in the world won't fix it. Thicker pieces of Salmon are best because you are less likely to overcook them.

## Directions

• Fillet Salmon using the deep-skin method, which is to remove the gray matter along with the skin and pluck the pin bones with needle-nose pliers or boning tweezers. If you are buying from your local fishmonger, ask to have the fillet deep-skinned as well.

• Wash planks and rub with olive oil.

• Combine brown sugar, Duke's Superb Herb Blend and Duke's Ready Anytime Seasoning in a bowl, and rub mixture on both sides of Wild Alaska Salmon

• Bake for approximately 8 minutes at 400 degrees.

• Serve with a side of Sinful Citrus Vinaigrette for dipping.

Note from Duke:

Coho Salmon, with its mild flavor and high Omega-3 fat content, works really well with these dishes. A few fun facts about Coho Salmon:

• Can swim up to 25 miles per hour

• Usually have a lifespan of four years

• Spawn in the same creeks or lakes where they were born

• Compared to King Salmon, they don't get very big. Mature adult Coho Salmon usually weigh between 6 and 12 pounds.

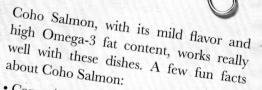

# SAVORY CHIPOTLE
# WILD ALASKA SALMON SANDWICH

You know when things come together and you think, "They were made for each other." Peanut butter and jelly, popcorn and butter, Romeo and Juliet. Well, this grouping is more of a threesome– rosemary bread, Wild Alaska Salmon, and our Hold Me Tight Chipotle Aioli. They were simply made for each other. Our rosemary bread is made by The Essential Baking Company and is the best I have ever tasted. It holds up to the chipotle peppers and complements the bold Wild Alaska Salmon flavor.

Serves one

## Ingredients

8 oz Wild Alaska Salmon fillet

large pinch Duke's Ready Anytime Seasoning (pg 323)

2 slices Essential Baking Company Rosemary Bread

1 Tbsp Let's Be Clarified Butter (pg 148)

½ cup Hold Me Tight Chipotle Aioli (pg 322)

¼ cup iceberg lettuce, shredded

2 tomato slices

¼ avocado, sliced and fanned

20 Sweet Treat Potato Fries (pg 259)

## Directions

• Fillet Salmon using the deep-skin method, which is to remove the gray matter along with the skin and pluck the pin bones with needle-nose pliers or boning tweezers. If you are buying from your local fishmonger, ask to have the fillet deep-skinned as well.

• Season both sides of the Salmon with Duke's Ready Anytime Seasoning.

• Grill both sides of the Salmon for 3-4 minutes per side or until fish has lost all its translucency.

• At the same time, on a flat-top grill or in a sauté pan, grill both slices of the rosemary bread in Let's Be Clarified Butter.

• Spread each slice of rosemary bread "coast to coast" with ¼ cup Hold Me Tight Chipotle Aioli.

• Add lettuce, avocado, tomato and cooked Salmon.

• Serve with remaining Hold Me Tight Chipotle Aioli for dipping the Sweet Treat Potato Fries or the sandwich itself.

# People Like That Are Hard To Find

The fishing business is very difficult. Risky, dangerous, and just plain ol' hard work. It's always a surprise when someone can survive long term in the business. One great story is Yakutat Seafoods run by Greg Indreland, operating owner along with partners Randy Patrick and Tab Goto. They almost didn't make it after a rough start in 2005, but their perseverance has paid off for our guests. They provide some of the best, if not the best, Coho Salmon in all of Alaska. As Greg describes it, "After the first year we started to focus on the fresh market because Yakutat fish are fresher than any others coming out of Alaska or Canada. With the help of Alaska Airlines, we started to gain traction in the market and the rest is history. We are in year eleven and count Duke's as one of our valued customers. Duke's has been using Yakutat gillnet Coho for those exact reasons mentioned, fresh and great quality."

Greg went on further to say, "Duke has come up in the past to see the plant, the fish, and meet the fishermen. He even got involved in going out in fishing skiffs to get the true feel for what the whole dynamic really is like. I like working with Duke because, like me, he believes in what he is doing and is personally invested financially, emotionally, and spiritually. People like that are hard to find these days. Which is why, in my opinion, we have a great working relationship. We are glad to be part of the new cookbook and a continuing relationship with Duke's."

This is one Duke you can dine with and forget all about the pomp and circumstance.

Because Duke Moscrip decided a long time ago that restaurants should be fun places to eat and drink. So each one of his four Chowder House locations makes you feel like royalty, but in a very casual way.

First, there's the food. Really good, simple preparations, just the way Duke likes to eat. The award-winning clam chowder, plus seven other chowders on the menu. The signature Casesar salad, Duke's great cheeseburger, crispy fish 'n chips, and a whole bunch of seafood items, all fit for a king.

Duke's Chowder House Restaurants are real lively, too. Not like some stuffy old castle.

And all of Duke's people make sure you feel right at home. Just like their Duke, they smile a lot and have a lot of fun waiting on you.

Duke's Restaurants are so much fun, in fact, and the food's so good, that the Duke himself eats there all the time.

Why, he might be sitting right next to you on your next visit.

So impress your friends. Tell 'em you've dined with a Duke.

Eat. Drink. Relax.

# When Was The Last Time You Ate With a Duke?

# Heavenly Halibut

It's what you'll eat in heaven.

# Fresh Isn't Fresh

Just like Salmon, fresh Halibut isn't really "fresh." As I wrote in the Salmon section of this cookbook, many years ago, I was shocked to learn that "fresh" fish isn't really fresh. It can take up to twenty-five days for Halibut to get from the ocean to most restaurants. Every Alaska Fisherman I've met only buys "frozen at the source" fish. Duke's Halibut is better than fresh because within forty-eight hours of capture, these beautiful whitefish are filleted, vacuum packed and frozen—which keeps the oxygen from affecting the flavor and texture, locking in that natural, fresh Halibut flavor. In blind taste-tests, frozen at the source Halibut wins over "fresh" every time.

The subtle and heavenly flavor of Halibut will drive you wild. Its meaty texture and almost nutty taste is the steak of the sea. Complementary to nearly any herbs, spices and juices, this amazing fish is a Northwest favorite, and I'm always excited to experience the next brilliant dish that Chef "Wild" Bill and I will dream up.

## Note from Duke: Crazy Halibut Facts to Impress Your Friends

- Halibut are dark brown on the top side with an off-white underbelly and have very small scales invisible to the naked eye embedded in their skin.

- At birth, they have an eye on each side of the head, and swim like a Salmon. After six months, one eye migrates to the other side so that there are two eyes on the same side, making them look more like flounder. At the same time, the stationary-eyed side darkens to match the top side, while the other side remains white. This color scheme disguises Halibut from above (blending with the ocean floor) and from below (blending into the light from the sky) and is known as countershading.

- Halibut never stop growing; the record so far is 578 pounds.

- Halibut rule the bottom of the ocean except when an Orca Whale wants to step in.

# "I Need To Be On The Boat"

Bob Simon of Pacific Seafood recalls our first meeting many years ago. "Duke met with me to discuss his vision of what he wanted to build. His goal was to serve high quality fish—what Pacific Seafood does best. Although I could explain to Duke why we were his best option, he wanted to see it for himself. He insisted that he go there, see it, touch it, and taste it. I said, 'Great. You want a tour of our plant, we do that all of the time.' Duke said, 'Bob, I want more than a plant tour. I need to be on the boat, with the skipper, talking, understanding, watching, and learning.' That was a tall order that I was not sure I could supply.

In the fishing industry, we do not let people on boats for safety and insurance reasons. I soon realized the only way to build our partnership was to give Duke what he requested. We managed to get Duke on a Salmon boat, Halibut boat, Rockfish boat, Shrimp boat, and a Crab boat. I was confident our mission was accomplished, but I was mistaken. Duke then requested to be in the processing plant, to look the plant manager in the eye and feel the commitment and integrity, to become a partner and team. Once again, we managed to fulfill his request. Duke now has a relationship with each manager in every facility that processes his fish."

Bob went on to say, "In an industry that sees both restaurants and seafood companies come and go, Duke has managed to build a special alliance for his restaurant guests that ensures an exceptional level of quality and trust with his suppliers. Duke and I recently had lunch together for a business review, and it was not long before guests in the restaurant recognized the name Pacific Seafood on my shirt and Duke's on his. The guests came up to the table to say, 'I don't know how you guys do it, but keep it going because the seafood is great!' These comments accentuate our goal."

Pacific Seafood is under the leadership of Frank Dulcich, the founder's namesake and grandson.

# BLACKBERRY FIELDS FOREVER HALIBUT gf

The Beatles may have changed the name of their famous tune had this little concoction been around in England back in the late 1960s. It also makes me wish blackberry season lasted forever because the unmistakable combination of sweet blackberries along with Halibut pull together to make your taste buds sing out loud with this delicious recipe. Just for the Halibut, you can also try raspberries, blueberries or peaches, as any of these fresh fruits dance a colorful dance with this fish. Don't worry; strawberries aren't the jealous type. They work, too.

Serves one

## Ingredients

8 oz Wild Alaska Halibut fillet

1 Tbsp extra virgin olive oil

large pinch Duke's Ready Anytime Seasoning (pg 323)

1 Tbsp fresh organic basil leaves, stems removed, diced small

12 fresh or frozen blackberries

2 Tbsp Amaretto

¼ cup chilled Darigold butter

## Directions

• Fillet Halibut using the deep-skin method, which is to remove the gray matter along with the skin. If you are buying from your local fishmonger, ask to have the fillet deep-skinned as well. Be sure to remove bones.

• Sprinkle Halibut with Duke's Ready Anytime Seasoning and pan-sear in olive oil on both sides until almost done (approximately 7 minutes).

• Add basil and blackberries (thaw before if frozen), and cook for 20 seconds; then deglaze with Amaretto (see Deglazing, Demystified, pg 326). After another 20 seconds, remove from heat (too much heat will separate the sauce), and swirl in butter until just incorporated.

• Serve Halibut with blackberries spooned over the top. Pour remaining blackberry pan juices into a small bowl and serve on the side.

# TEMPTING THAI GINGER HALIBUT gf

These exotic Asian flavors combine together to bring you a little spice wrapped up in a beautifully easy to prepare dish. One bite and your taste buds will be tempted to finish the whole thing.

Serves one

## Ingredients

8 oz Wild Alaska Halibut fillet

1 Tbsp Duke's Superb Herb Blend (pg 322)

large pinch Duke's Ready Anytime Seasoning (pg 323)

1 Tbsp Lct's Bc Clarified Butter (pg 148)

1 Tbsp extra virgin olive oil

2 tsp fresh organic basil leaves, stems removed, diced small

½ cup spinach leaves, diced small

6 Tbsp Incredibly Healthy Vegetable Stock (pg 326)

¾ cup Spicy Coconut Broth (below)

1 Tbsp toasted macadamia nuts

## Directions

• Fillet Halibut using the deep-skin method, which is to remove the gray matter along with the skin. If you are buying from your local fishmonger, ask to have the fillet deep-skinned as well. Be sure to remove bones.

• Sprinkle one side of Halibut with Duke's Ready Anytime Seasoning and Duke's Superb Herb Blend, and on a hot, flat griddle, or sauté pan, brown Halibut seasoned-side down in Let's Be Clarified Butter. Cook for 3-4 minutes per side until fish has lost all its translucency.

• At the same time, in a saucepan, sauté spinach and basil in olive oil until wilted. Add vegetable stock and coconut broth. Bring to a boil.

• Pour mixture into a bowl and place Halibut on top. Garnish with toasted macadamia nuts.

# SPICY COCONUT BROTH gf

## Ingredients

1 Tbsp Thai One On Sweet Chili Sauce (pg 279)

2 Tbsp macadamia nuts, diced small

1 Tbsp puréed ginger (available in grocery stores)

½ tsp celery salt

2 tsp fresh lime juice

1 tsp lime zest from a lime zester

½ tsp sugar in the raw

½ tsp extra virgin olive oil

½ tsp sesame oil

½ cup coconut milk

## Directions

• In a heavy-gauged pan, cook all broth ingredients at 170 degrees for 10 minutes, stirring occasionally until evenly incorporated.

# DUNGENESS CRAB STUFFED JUST FOR THE HALIBUT

This Chef "Wild" Bill original has been with us since he started working with me at Duke's back in 1996, and it has been on the menu ever since. What's not to love? Beautiful, meaty Halibut with a surprise of rich, decadent Dungeness Crabmeat inside. This was a favorite of Bill's Mom, Gail, who ordered it all the time. Sometimes you can still catch Bill enjoying this dish with a glass of Chardonnay after a busy shift in the kitchen.

Serves one

## Ingredients

8 oz Wild Alaska Halibut fillet

6 Tbsp It's Sooo Good Seafood Stuffing (pg 329)

1 Tbsp breadcrumbs

¼ cup Incredibly Healthy Vegetable Stock (pg 326)

¼ cup Fill Me Up Buttercup Butta Cream Sauce (pg 149)

## Directions

- Preheat oven to 425 degrees.

- Fillet Halibut using the deep-skin method, which is to remove the gray matter along with the skin. If you are buying from your local fishmonger, ask to have the fillet deep-skinned as well. Be sure to remove bones.

- Cut a "pocket" into fillet as follows: Lay the fillet on a cutting board. Without cutting through the fillet, start from the top corner and cut diagonally on the bias into the fish 2½ inches deep.

- Place Halibut in a baking pan. Add stuffing to the pocket (some of the stuffing will be showing outside the fillet). Sprinkle breadcrumbs over the exposed stuffing, which will turn crisp and golden brown when cooked.

- Slowly add vegetable stock to baking pan, being careful not to get the breadcrumbs wet.

- Bake for 8 minutes or until fish has lost all its translucency. (Time varies depending on thickness. Don't be afraid to slightly tear open the edge of the fillet with a fork to check it.)

- Serve on a puddle of warmed Fill Me Up Buttercup Butta Cream Sauce.

# HALIBUT FORTUNATO gf

Halibut is easily substituted for Salmon in this original recipe inspired by Chef Monique Barbeau (see Salmon Fortunato recipe, pg 192). Not unlike the Salmon, you'll be the fortunate one when you taste this amazing creation.

Serves one

## Ingredients

8 oz Wild Alaska Halibut fillet

1 Tbsp extra virgin olive oil

¼ cup Sundried Tomato Relish (pg 329)

12 pine nuts

## Directions

- Fillet Halibut using the deep-skin method, which is to remove the gray matter along with the skin. If you are buying from your local fishmonger, ask to have the fillet deep-skinned as well. Be sure to remove bones.

- Cook Halibut in a sauté pan on medium-high heat for 3-4 minutes per side or until fish has lost all its translucency. To check doneness, place a spatula under fish about halfway and lift until the fillet breaks open. It's okay to have a small crack in the surface; better to have the correct doneness than a pretty fillet that is raw or overdone. The trick to Halibut is not to overcook it because it can get very dry.

- Spoon Sundried Tomato Relish over Halibut and sprinkle with pine nuts.

# HOLY HALIBUT MACADAMIA

This was voted "Best new seafood entrée in Seattle" by me. So what if I was the only voter? It was absolutely true when we first served it, and now I think it most likely moved to the "Most epic seafood entrée in Seattle." The beurre blanc with the addition of hazelnut syrup renders a taste similar to butterscotch. As a kid, butterscotch was it, and I often wonder what ever happened to it. I think it was overtaken by caramel for some reason. Nevertheless, this recipe brings it back and mingles beautifully with the nutty, smooth-textured macadamias.

Serves one

## Ingredients

8 oz Wild Alaska Halibut fillet

¼ cup Macadamia Nut Breading (below)

2 Tbsp Let's Be Clarified Butter (pg 148)

¼ cup I Love Hazelnut Butta Cream Sauce (pg 149)

egg wash (one whole egg beaten with a small splash of water)

 Tip from Chef "Wild" Bill:

Check for doneness by sliding a spatula under fish about halfway and lift up slightly. Look for no translucency all the way through the middle of the fillet. The trick to Halibut is not to overcook because it can get very dry.

## Directions

- Fillet Halibut using the deep-skin method, which is to remove the gray matter along with the skin. If you are buying from your local fishmonger, ask to have the fillet deep-skinned as well. Be sure to remove bones.

- Place Halibut on a cutting board and blot fish with a paper towel to remove excess moisture. Brush top of fillet with 1 Tbsp egg wash and firmly press macadamia nut breading onto fish.

- On a flat griddle or sauté pan, heat Let's Be Clarified Butter and grill Halibut nut-side down until the macadamia mixture is golden brown (approximately 3-4 minutes). Flip and continue to cook for another 3-4 minutes until fish has lost all its translucency.

- Serve on a puddle of warmed I Love Hazelnut Butta Cream Sauce.

# MACADAMIA NUT BREADING

## Ingredients

½ lb macadamia nuts

1 cup Duke's Crunchy Croutons (pg 328)

½ bunch parsley, stems removed

½ cup Parmesan cheese and ½ cup Asiago cheese, grated and combined

## Directions

- In a food processor, purée Duke's Crunchy Croutons. Add parsley leaves, and blend until finely chopped. Add macadamia nuts and cheeses, and pulse until macadamias are a coarse grind. Keep refrigerated.

# It's So Dreamy Parmesan Halibut

It's so dreamy because you'll think you were dreaming. This dish is that amazing. The subtle taste of capers combine with the cheese in this recipe to deliver a perfect bite without overwhelming the delicate Halibut flavor.

Serves one

## Ingredients

8 oz Wild Alaska Halibut fillet

large pinch Duke's Ready Anytime Seasoning (pg 323)

egg wash (one egg beaten with a small splash of water)

2 Tbsp Parmesan cheese plus 2 Tbsp Asiago cheese, grated and combined

¼ cup panko breadcrumbs (available at most grocery stores)

2 Tbsp Let's Be Clarified Butter (pg 148)

¼ cup Fill Me Up Buttercup Butta Cream Sauce (pg 149)

12 capers

## Directions

• Fillet Halibut using the deep-skin method, which is to remove the gray matter along with the skin. If you are buying from your local fishmonger, ask to have the fillet deep-skinned as well. Be sure to remove bones.

• Sprinkle Halibut with Duke's Ready Anytime Seasoning, and then brush with 1 Tbsp egg wash.

• Cover both sides of fish with cheese mixture and panko breadcrumbs. Cook until golden brown, about 3-4 minutes per side or until fish has lost all its translucency.

• Serve on a warmed puddle of Fill Me Up Buttercup Butta Cream Sauce and sprinkle with capers.

# BLACKENED HAPPY HALIBUT SANDWICH

This is a quick and easy recipe that is sure to bring a smile to your face. Perfectly blackened Halibut with fresh ingredients carefully placed on a Nearly Brioche Burger Bun. There's only love to be had . . . toasty, halibutty, buttery love.

Serves one

## Ingredients

8 oz Wild Alaska Halibut fillet

generous pinch Blackening Spice Of Life (pg 323)

1 tsp Let's Be Clarified Butter (pg 148)

1 organic burger bun (we use Essential Baking Company Nearly Brioche Burger Buns)

¼ cup Hold Me Tight Chipotle Aioli (pg 322)

¼ cup shredded lettuce

1 tomato slice

¼ cup Walla Walla Sweet Haystack Onion Straws (pg 286)

## Directions

- Fillet Halibut using the deep-skin method, which is to remove the gray matter along with the skin. If you are buying from your local fishmonger, ask to have the fillet deep-skinned as well. Be sure to remove bones.

- Add Blackening Spice Of Life to Halibut on one side only.

- On a hot, flat griddle or sauté pan, grill Halibut in Let's Be Clarified Butter for 3-4 minutes per side or until fish has lost all its translucency. (Halibut overcooks easily so watch carefully) While Halibut is cooking, grill the bun for approximately 3-4 minutes.

- Place Halibut on bottom bun. Spread a dollop of Hold Me Tight Chipotle Aioli liberally on the top bun; then add lettuce, tomato and Walla Walla Sweet Haystack Onion Straws. Serve with remaining aioli on the side for dipping.

# Wet & Wild Seafood

So good it jumps
in your mouth.

# ALL KINDS OF WEATHERVANE ALASKA SCALLOPS RAVIOLI

Ravioli, the pillows of Italy, marries together with the pillows of the sea. It lays to rest any doubts of this not being the most amazing ravioli dish you've ever had. We have seen many a guest swoon over our seafood, but this particular recipe earns many an "Oh, My God" statement bordering on a revelation.

Serves one

## Ingredients

7 large Alaska Weathervane Scallops

2 Tbsp Duke's Ready Anytime Seasoning (pg 323)

4 Tbsp extra virgin olive oil

7 fresh raviolis (use your favorite stuffing–Duke's uses pumpkin and mascarpone stuffed)

2 Tbsp fresh tomatoes, diced

pinch Duke's Superb Herb Blend (pg 322)

pinch fresh organic basil leaves, stems removed, diced small

1 tsp fresh garlic, diced small

6 Roasted Garlic Cloves (pg 328)

2 Tbsp white wine

¼ cup chilled Darigold butter

## Directions

- Prepare raviolis first, they take longer. Blanch raviolis in salted boiling water until they float, about 5 minutes (7 minutes for frozen). Drain and set aside.

- Toss raviolis in a small amount of olive oil to prevent them from sticking together.

- Pat Scallops dry and sprinkle with Duke's Ready Anytime Seasoning.

- Heat 2 Tbsp olive oil on a flat griddle or sauté pan and sear Scallops on both sides until golden brown for approximately 2-3 minutes per side.

- In a separate pan, heat remaining 2 Tbsp olive oil and sauté tomatoes, Duke's Superb Herb Blend, basil, garlic and roasted garlic for 2 minutes.

- Deglaze with white wine (Deglazing, Demystified, pg 326). Add cooked raviolis (for best results, raviolis should not sit longer than a minute before joining the sauce). Add butter and swirl until incorporated.

- Create a circle of raviolis on the plate and drizzle with sauce. Top each ravioli with one Scallop.

# Tender, Succulent, Sweet, What Could Be Better?

"Wild" Bill and I occasionally go on R & D (research and development) sojourns. One such outing years ago yielded the best tasting Scallops on the planet. We attended a waterfront festival in Ballard surrounded by fishing boats. We met Jim Stone, his wife Mona, and his fellow Scallop fishermen and partners who were cooking and serving their tender Scallops. As Jim puts it, "Duke and Bill loved the sweet taste of the pan-seared Weathervane Scallops we were serving." It didn't take us but a few seconds to realize that their Alaska Weathervane Scallops were incredible.

But Jim didn't stop there. "Just having the sweetest Scallops in the world on his menu wasn't enough for Duke, though. He had to know every detail of how, when, and where the Scallop fishermen do what they do. So the next thing we knew, Duke was flying into Yakutat, Alaska and jumping onboard the 124' fishing vessel *Provider* and going out for a day with Captain Tom Minio and crew to learn everything. Since then, Duke has become like an uncle, not only to the *Provider* crew, but to all of us from the other boats. Uncle Duke is also never afraid to give us constructive criticism if he sees any quality issue slip even just a little. This helps us keep our quality top-notch. Duke is exactly the type of restaurateur we love to work with, so much more rewarding for fishermen than just dealing with seafood distributors and never knowing where our Weathervanes go."

I feel very privileged to have been able to fish with the fishermen on the *Provider*. I saw what few restaurant owners get to see and experience. The vessels catch, shuck, clean, size-sort, box, and rapid-deep-freeze the Alaska Weathervane within four short hours of capture. This process allows them to lock in the Weathervane's natural sweet flavor and delicate texture. The Scallops are never adulterated with chemicals as is done to so many other varieties of Scallops worldwide. I know firsthand why these Scallops are the best in the world. And, notably, the Scallops are fished sustainably in a manner respectful of the environment and other fisheries.

TASTE THE DIFFERENCE

WILD ALASKA
WEATHERVANE SCALLOPS
ALASKASCALLOP.NET

Duke admiring a Weathervane Scallop in the wild.

# Little Ship Of Heaven

## By Chef "Wild" Bill Ranniger

When I was a kid, my family towed a sinking houseboat they'd gotten for free to a plot of land on Henry Island in the San Juan Islands. Using winches and cut logs as rollers, we got the boat on shore, and it became our family cabin.

At the age of ten, I would go fishing in our little fourteen-foot aluminum boat by myself early in the morning, as nobody wanted to go as often as I did. Rockfish and Ling Cod were fairly easy to catch back in those days. I would fillet the fish and then use the bones, fins and guts for bait in my crab pots. After securing the fish to the bottom of the pot (otherwise, the bait floats to the top, and the crab will just eat from the top of the pot and crawl off with it when you start hauling it in), I would get back into my trusty boat and head to Westcott Bay. We called it Dungeness Bay because of how plentiful the crab was there. I would drop my pots and leave them to soak all night, then head for home, dreaming all the way of fresh Dungeness.

I could barely sleep at night after a crab pot drop. We called it a "Christmas Morning Pull" as we first started tugging on the rope and hauling those first pots in anxiously awaiting a loaded pot full of delicious Dungeness. Some pots are full and some empty, but then it's always onto the next pot to see what's there. After sorting all the crabs, freeing the women and children, counting all my fingers to make sure nothing was lost along the way, it was time to share the harvest.

I used to be afraid of these tasty dudes, with their funky little eyes, barbed legs and claws. They are pretty intimidating looking, and if you get your finger in the way of their pinchers, it can leave a pretty serious mark. Crabs need to be cooked alive, so as soon as I got back to shore, I boiled up a big pot of saltwater, looked the crab in the eyes and lied to them. I told them it was a hot tub party and dropped them in.

After cooking them up, we always enjoyed them cold with melted butter. When we had company, we would make fresh garlic or lemon butter, but I have always liked mine with straight pure, melted butter. We'd spread out yesterday's newspapers, give everyone a hammer to crack the shells and just go for it. The fish I caught was usually made into Fish and Chips accompanied with good tartar and cocktail sauce. Along with the crab, this made a feast fit for the gods, and our little cabin on the shore felt like a Little Ship of Heaven.

# DUNGENESS CRAB "UN" CAKES

From Chef "Wild" Bill: As you can tell from my childhood story (pg 237), I have always loved Crab. The first Crab cakes I put on the menu at Duke's had all of these great local ingredients, including Washington Granny Smith apples, Walla Walla Sweet onions and sourdough bread. They were good, but I never revered them. I didn't think they were "great." Duke and I decided to go on "The Great Crab Cake Quest." We made a list of the best seafood restaurants in the city and vowed to find the best. Our first night out, we visited eight different restaurants, eating Crab cakes and sampling wine like it was going out of style (not a bad night of work!). That night, we didn't find one single Crab cake we could say was "great." A lot of "good" Crab cakes, but we already had a "good" Crab cake at Duke's; we wanted great, epic Crab cakes. We commenced our quest the following evening and hit six more restaurants, devouring Crab cakes and more wine. Still settling on the fact that everything we'd tried was fine but not great, Duke turned to me and said, "You know what's great about Crab cakes? Crab! You know what's terrible? Cake!" And thus, our GREAT Crab "Un"Cakes were born. It was like returning back to my roots. I remembered as a boy that I only liked my Crab with straight, pure melted butter and no filler. We use absolutely no breading in our "Un"Cakes, and they are one of the most popular things we serve at Duke's. Food for thought: "Don't go over-complicating something that's already delicious!"

Makes Ten 3 oz "Un"Cakes

## Ingredients

1¼ lbs fresh Dungeness Crabmeat

½ bunch green onions, green parts only, diced small

1 tsp Duke's Superb Herb Blend (pg 322)

½ cup Hold Me Tight Chipotle Aioli (pg 322)

1 cup + 2 Tbsp Zesty Lusty Lime Aioli (pg 321)

2 Tbsp fresh organic basil leaves, stems removed, diced small

2 Tbsp fresh organic parsley, stems removed, diced small

2 organic eggs

3 cups panko breadcrumbs (available at most grocery stores)

2 Tbsp Let's Be Clarified Butter (pg 148)

## Directions

- Squeeze excess liquid from Crab and place in a bowl. Add green onions, Duke's Superb Herb Blend, Hold Me Tight Chipotle Aioli, 1 cup of Zesty Lusty Lime Aioli, herbs, eggs, and mix well.

- Ball into 3 oz portions (like making a snowball). Lightly press into panko breadcrumbs and flatten into ½ inch thick discs.

- Refrigerate for at least 1 hour before cooking. (This helps them hold together.)

- On a flat griddle or sauté pan, heat Let's Be Clarified Butter to medium-high. Grill Dungeness Crab "Un"Cake until golden brown for approximately 3-4 minutes per side (be careful, they are delicate to work with). Serve with remaining Zesty Lusty Lime Aioli.

 Tip from Chef "Wild" Bill:
The breadcrumbs are only for the outer crust, there are NO breadcrumbs in the Crab mixture. They are a bit fragile so handle them carefully.

# DUNGENESS CRAB LOVER'S CLUB

This combination will leave you wondering what a club really ever was. If you love Dungeness, then this is the club for you. With Dungeness Crab piled high atop Essential Baking Company Rosemary Bread combined with avocados, tomatoes and Jarlsberg Swiss cheese, you'll wonder whether there's a membership fee for it.

Serves one

## Ingredients

¼ cup fresh Dungeness Crabmeat

2 tsp Ocean Fresh Dressing (pg 135)

2 slices Essential Baking Company Rosemary Bread

¼ avocado, sliced thin

2 slices tomato

2 slices Jarlsberg Swiss cheese

2 Tbsp Let's Be Clarified Butter (pg 148)

## Directions

• Squeeze excess liquid from Crab and place in a small bowl. Mix Crab with Ocean Fresh Dressing. Spread on 1 slice of rosemary bread.

• Top the other piece of bread with 1 slice of cheese and grill bread-side down in Let's Be Clarified Butter until golden brown, approximately 3-4 minutes.

• Top the Crab with the second slice of cheese and grill bread-side down until golden brown, approximately 3-4 minutes. Add avocado and tomato slices.

• Match bread slices together and slice in half diagonally.

# STUFFED AND PUFFED PRAWNS

This dish was originally created by Alan Caraco, our former Chef at Duke's in Bellevue in the early 1990s, and it has been a menu favorite ever since. These guys are all puffed up and prepped to punch you with flavors that will blow your mind.

serves four

## Ingredients

24 Wild Mexican Prawns (size 21-25 per lb), peeled and deveined

1 cup Fill Me Up Buttercup Butta Cream Sauce (pg 149)

¼ cup Basil Almond Pretty Pesto (pg 320)

1 batch It's Sooo Good Seafood Stuffing (pg 329)

¼ cup white wine

## Directions

- Remove the shells. Leave the tails on for looks. Devein Prawns from the belly side, not the top which is the usual method. The reason is that, although the vein is on the top side, we need to create a place for the stuffing in the belly and the vein can be reached from the underside and removed. The tail curls up and creates a perfect pocket in the belly so we must make our cut on the underside, remove the vein and then stuff the belly. Make a small slice, about 2 inches, on the underside of the Shrimp.

- Stuff each Prawn with 2 Tbsp It's Sooo Good Seafood Stuffing.

- Place stuffed Prawns in a baking dish and add wine to the bottom.

- Bake at 425 degrees for 8 minutes or until Prawns have lost their translucency (or their internal temperature reaches 130 degrees). Stuffing should be golden brown.

- Make a puddle of Fill Me Up Buttercup Butta Cream Sauce on a plate with a dollop of Basil Almond Pretty Pesto to accent the flavor.

- With a metal spatula, place Prawns on sauce.

# HANKY PANKY ORANGE PRAWNS gf

A foodie friend of mine, Carol Pierce, cooked something very similar to this for me, and I was blown away by the pairing of orange and Prawns. Sometimes, the simplest combinations are right under our noses, literally. This was a great discovery, and it is very simple to execute. Caution: It may make you a little frisky.

Serves two

## Ingredients

14 Wild Mexican Prawns (size 21-25 per lb), peeled and deveined

2 Tbsp extra virgin olive oil

2 Tbsp fresh organic basil leaves, diced small

20 small Candy Dandy Orange Peels (pg 338)

½ cup orange-flavored liqueur (Grand Marnier or Cointreau)

½ cup Darigold butter

pinch Duke's Ready Anytime Seasoning (pg 323)

## Directions

• Sauté Prawns in olive oil until almost done, 2-3 minutes per side.

• Deglaze with Grand Marnier (Deglazing, Demystified, pg 326).

• Add Candy Dandy Orange Peels and basil; then immediately remove from heat and swirl in butter. Garnish with extra Candy Dandy Orange Peels.

**DukeWorthy™ Provider**

## "Shrimp Boats Are A Coming, We're Dancing Tonight"

Dow-Li Kou of Aqua Star, who provides us with Wild Mexican Prawns, said recently, "Whereas with most customers, we focused on the logistics of the business, but with Duke we focused our meetings on gaining an in-depth understanding of the story behind each piece of seafood that would be served at his restaurants."

The Wild Mexican Prawns come from the Sea of Cortez near Guayamas and are enriched with a fertile and food-friendly environment. The Prawns are captured, head and body removed, and frozen immediately. This guarantees the fresh-tasting quality. I have tasted Prawns from all over the world. I have never had a more consistent, firm, and fresh-tasting Prawn than these Wild Mexican Prawns provided by Aqua Star. They have a clean taste with a pure Prawn aroma that can only come from a superior resource with excellent seafood handling. All of the boats catching their Prawns are equipped with TEDs (Turtle Excluder Devices), and they practice sustainability to ensure the needs of the future.

*AquaStar*®

# PRAWNS PASTA PRETTY PESTO

Prawns . . . Pasta . . . Pesto—now this is a trifecta that will fire up your taste buds and make you sing . . . or at least make them do a little dance in your mouth. These flavor combinations make this pasta dish unbelievable. Pesto seems to go with everything.

Serves one

## Ingredients

5 Wild Mexican Prawns (size 21-25 per lb), peeled and deveined

¾ cup premium or fresh-made corkscrew pasta (we use Barilla brand)

2 Tbsp extra virgin olive oil

1 Tbsp fresh garlic, diced small

3 asparagus spears, white stocks removed, sliced into 1-inch sections

1 cup Darigold heavy whipping cream (the higher the butterfat, the better)

¼ cup Duke's Basil Almond Pretty Pesto (pg 320)

pinch Duke's Ready Anytime Seasoning (pg 323)

1 Tbsp Parmesan cheese and 1 Tbsp Asiago cheese, grated and combined

14 toasted pine nuts

## Directions

- Prepare pasta first, it takes longer. Blanch pasta in boiling salted water to al dente (approximately 12 minutes); then run under cold water to cool. You can do this well ahead of time.

- In a large sauté pan, heat olive oil and add Prawns, garlic and asparagus, and sauté for 3 minutes until Prawns are almost done.

- Add cream, Basil Almond Pretty Pesto and Duke's Ready Anytime Seasoning. Reduce to about half or desired thickness (approximately 3-4 more mintues).

- Add pasta and toss evenly to coat. Garnish with grated cheese mixture and toasted pine nuts.

# BOMBAY BICYCLE CLUB PRAWNS  gf

I have heard that there's a secret club in India that is so exclusive the members can only ride bicycles to get to it. You'll have no trouble finding the flavor here.

Serves six

## Ingredients

30 Wild Mexican Prawns (size 21-25 per lb), peeled and deveined

3 medium butternut squash, washed and sliced in half lengthwise

3 Tbsp extra virgin olive oil

2 Tbsp + pinch Duke's Ready Anytime Seasoning (pg 323)

2 Tbsp fresh garlic, diced small

pinch red pepper flakes (if you like heat)

pinch Duke's Superb Herb Blend (pg 322)

½ tsp curry powder (Duke's uses a "Madras Blend," which is a little hot)

½ cup coconut milk

2 Tbsp Garlic Lover's Butter (pg 148)

## Directions

- Prepare squash first, it takes longer. Preheat oven to 350 degrees. Using an ice cream scoop, scrape out squash seeds. Fill a roasting pan with 2 cups of water and place squash face-up in water. Drizzle squash with half the olive oil, and sprinkle with 2 Tbsp Duke's Ready Anytime Seasoning. Cover pan with foil, airtight.

- Roast squash at 350 degrees for about 50 minutes or until squash is soft to the touch. Remove foil and continue to roast squash for 5 more minutes. Place each half on a plate.

- Heat remaining olive oil in a large sauté pan over medium-high heat. Add Prawns and cook halfway, about 1½ minutes per side. The Prawns will be mostly "white" in color.

- Add fresh garlic and sauté for an additional minute.

- Then, all at once, add red pepper, Duke's Superb Herb Blend, curry powder and a pinch of Duke's Ready Anytime Seasoning. Cook for about a minute more.

- Deglaze with coconut milk (Deglazing, Demystified, pg 326). Bring to boil and swirl in Garlic Lover's Butter until evenly incorporated.

- Place 5 Prawns into each squash "bowl." Distribute most of the pan sauces evenly over squashes, but reserve a small amount for dipping.

 Tip from Chef "Wild" Bill:

Curry powder is actually a blend of up to twenty different spices and can vary quite a bit, depending on the "blender" and its origin. The spices most commonly used are cardamom, chilies, cloves, cinnamon, poppy seeds, sesame seeds, fenugreek, mace, nutmeg, red and black peppers, saffron (this is an expensive ingredient and is often omitted), tamarind and turmeric. The blends found in India, curry's birthplace, are quite different than the ones found in spice racks in the USA. If you have the opportunity to try the Indian-origin curries, I highly recommend it. Caution: Some can be very, very hot.

# LICK YOUR PLATE LING COD gf

Bruce Gore, legendary fisherman and inventor of "Frozen At Sea" Salmon Processing, provided Duke's with our first Ling Cod. When we cooked him this dish, he all but licked the plate and asked for another one. True story. He liked it that much! This is another dish that I literally dreamed up. Sambuca just seemed the right thing with Ling Cod.

Serves one

## Ingredients

8 oz Ling Cod

½ cup seasoned flour mix [7 Tbsp flour or Duke's Gluten-Free Flour Blend (pg 174) + 1½ tsp Kosher salt and 1½ tsp fresh cracked pepper]

2 Tbsp extra virgin olive oil

¼ cup Sambuca liqueur

pinch Duke's Superb Herb Blend (pg 322)

6 Tbsp Fill Me Up Buttercup Butta Cream Sauce (pg 149)

## Directions

- Fillet Ling Cod using the deep-skin method, which is to remove the gray matter along with the skin. If you are buying from your local fishmonger, ask to have the fillet deep-skinned as well. Be sure to remove all bones.

- Preheat oven to 400 degrees.

- In a sauté pan, heat olive oil on high but do not smoke.

- Dredge Ling Cod in seasoned flour mix and cook until golden brown on both sides, approximately 2 minutes per side.

- Deglaze with Sambuca (Deglazing, Demystified pg 326).

- Cook in 400-degree oven until fish has lost all translucency, about 4 minutes.

- Remove pan and let it sit for 1 minute; then sprinkle Duke's Superb Herb Blend over fish.

- Swirl in Fill Me Up Buttercup Butta Cream Sauce.

- With a spatula remove Ling Cod and place on plate.

- Drizzle liquid from pan on top of Ling Cod.

# THE POPE'S SEAFOOD CIOPPINO

Note from Chef "Wild" Bill: A heap of thanks to the Italian immigrants from San Francisco who are credited for bringing this recipe to the States. If you have odds and ends from filleting your catch, this is an amazing use for them. For example, in the summer, I fish at a spot near Westport and save the trim from whatever I catch, whether it's Ling Cod, Rockfish or Salmon. Then, I buy Shrimp, Clams, Mussels and Dungeness Crab from my local fishmonger. Don't ever worry about the amounts or having a specific variety because this recipe works well with whatever you have on hand as long as it's fresh and high quality. This is honestly one of my family's favorite meals. It is full of ingredients that are good for the heart and mind. This recipe also contains no gluten or dairy, as long as the bread that accompanies is also gluten-free, keeping it on the "lighter" side.

Serves one

## Ingredients

¼ cup Alaska whitefish or fresh local whitefish (Halibut, Cod, Rockfish) diced medium

¼ cup Wild Alaska Salmon or fresh local Salmon, diced medium

3 large Wild Mexican Prawns (size 21-25 per lb), peeled and deveined

6 fresh Penn Cove Mussels

1 Tbsp extra virgin olive oil

1 cup + 2 Tbsp North by Northwest Seafood Chowder Base (pg 160)

1 tsp fresh organic basil leaves, stems removed, diced small

2 Tbsp Dungeness Crabmeat (or in the shell)

## Directions

• Fillet seafood using the deep-skin method, which is to remove the gray matter along with the skin and pluck the bones and pin bones of Salmon with your fingers or with needle-nose pliers or boning tweezers if necessary. If you are buying from your local fishmonger, ask to have the fillet deep-skinned as well.

• In olive oil, sauté Salmon, whitefish, Prawns and Mussels in a large sauté pan until they are half-done (approximately 3-4 minutes).

• Add North by Northwest Seafood Chowder Base and basil.

• Cook until seafood is cooked through and Mussels have opened (liquid is at least 145 degrees) about 4 minutes.

• Add Crab to other seafood just before serving.

 Tip from Chef "Wild" Bill:

If Crab is added too early, it will break down and become stringy. You only need to get it warm at the end of the cooking process. Serves one very hungry person.

# Tasty Fish & Chips

will put a smile
on your face.

# OH MY COD! FISH & CHIPS AND HER MAJESTY HALIBUT & CHIPS

You're Darn Right, Oh My Cod! These are a pure delight for two reasons. First, my favorite beer, Mac & Jack's African Amber, is added to the batter fresh from the tap. Second is the outstanding taste of our True Cod, which arrives on your plate after a tightly-linked chain of events that preserve its freshness and taste. As soon as the Cod is harvested from the icy, clear waters of Alaska, the fish are transferred to a holding tank beneath the deck filled with refrigerated sea water (RSW) and delivered to the processor within days of the catch. The processor, Trident Seafoods, fillets, vacuum packs and freezes the fish immediately. They also take the additional step of selecting only the Cod loin, which is the best part of the fish. Sure, we could buy twice-frozen Cod from China. It's cheaper, but it tastes like cardboard, and it is usually soaked with an inorganic compound called tripolyphosphate. Why get toxic cardboard when you can enjoy tasty, 100 percent True Cod. Many of our guests also love Her Majesty Halibut and Chips, named for their exalted status in the fish world. The recipe following works with either Halibut or Cod.

Serves two

## Ingredients

12 oz Alaska True Cod or Wild Alaska Halibut

Friday's Child Fish Breading (pg 258)

2 cups panko breadcrumbs

1 cup Give Me More Tartar Sauce (pg 259)

4 medium organic yellow potatoes (for fries)

GMO-free canola oil, for frying

1 cup Duke's Coltrane Coleslaw (pg 280)

3 oz Organic or All Natural Heinz Ketchup
(make your own or purchase one made with
no high fructose corn syrup)

## Directions

- See the following pages for complete steps and directions.

Note from uke:

Try Her Majesty Halibut & Chips with Nothing But Blue Sky Bleu Cheese Dressing (pg 139) instead of Give Me More Tartar Sauce. It's so delicious that maybe they should call it Nothing But "Royal" Bleu Cheese Dressing!

## Fish & Chips, Step One

- Fillet your Cod or Halibut using the deep-skin method, which is to remove the gray matter along with the skin. If you are buying from your local fishmonger, ask to have the fillet deep-skinned as well. Be sure to remove all bones.

- Cut fish in 2 oz portions.

- Dry fish portions with paper towels, preferably an hour or more in advance to enable the batter and breading to adhere better.

- Dip fish in Friday's Child Fish Breading and allow excess to drip; then coat in panko until evenly coated (panko is the key to keeping it light). Place in one single layer on a plate or platter, and set aside while you make the fries and tartar sauce.

## Fish & Chips, Step Two

- Add enough oil to a Dutch oven or thick-sided soup pot to submerge fish completely. Using a candy or oil thermometer to check temperature, heat oil to 350 degrees. Be very careful—adjust oil temperature slowly. If the oil is too hot, it will overcook the breading and the fish will be undercooked. If the oil isn't hot enough, the breading will be soggy.

- Fry fish in oil until golden brown, about 4 minutes each side or until fish has an internal temperature of 145 degrees. Don't be afraid to check the doneness by cutting into the side of the fillet with a fork. (Perfectly cooked fish takes priority over appearances any day.)

- Serve hot with fries, Duke's Coltrane Coleslaw, Give Me More Tartar Sauce and Organic or All Natural Heinz Ketchup.

# FRIDAY'S CHILD FISH BREADING

## Ingredients

½ cup tempura batter (available at most grocery stores)

¾ bottle (9 oz) your favorite beer (because this is thirsty work, the unused quarter of a beer goes to the chef)

1½ tsp Duke's Ready Anytime Seasoning (pg 323)

## Directions

- Mix all ingredients with a whisk until smooth.

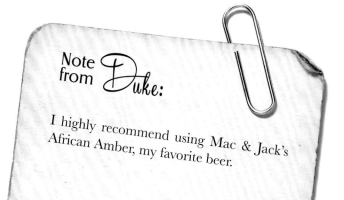

Note from *Duke:*

I highly recommend using Mac & Jack's African Amber, my favorite beer.

# "GIVE ME MORE TARTAR SAUCE" gf

This request is something we hear often at Duke's after people taste our tartar sauce. It seems simple to make, but most tartar sauces are surprisingly mundane. Capers are the key ingredient; they balance the sauce for the right amount of tart and sweet.

Makes 8-10 servings for two 3 oz. portions of fish

## Ingredients

2½ cups Make It Yourself Mayo (pg 320) or buy one made with olive oil

½ cup dill pickle relish (we use local Pleasant Valley)

6 Tbsp fresh Walla Walla Sweet onion, diced

2 Tbsp fresh squeezed lemon juice

1½ Tbsp Italian or Spanish capers

1½ Tbsp white pepper

2 Tbsp parsley, stems removed

1½ tsp Lea & Perrins Worcestershire Sauce

2 Tbsp fresh organic dill, stems removed

## Directions

• In a food processor, blend everything except for the mayonnaise thoroughly. Hand-mix mayonnaise until evenly incorporated. Keep chilled. This keeps for up to two weeks in the refrigerator.

# FISH OR CUT BAIT FRENCH FRIES

We recommend organic yellow potatoes, but play around with different varieties to see what you like best. Slice potatoes lengthwise into ¼-inch-thick ovals, then into ¼-inch-wide sticks, and run under cold water to release excess starch.

• Drain in a colander and dry completely by laying side-by-side between paper towels—water on the potatoes will make them "jump" in the hot oil which is a burn hazard.

• Fry in hot oil in a Dutch oven or thick-sided soup pot until golden brown.

• Using a spiderweb ladle, place potatoes on a sheet pan in a 200 degree oven while you fry the fish.

 Tip from Chef "Wild" Bill:

Sweet Treat Potato Fries made from sliced sweet potatoes are also a nice change of flavor and pace.

# A Family of Fishermen

Chuck Bundrant, Chairman and Founder of Trident Seafoods, has sold us seafood since the early '70s. The Bundrants are truly A Family Of Fishermen . . . From The Source To The Plate Since 1973.

Unlike other seafood corporations that are owned by investment bankers, Trident Seafoods is family owned and proud of it. Unlike other seafood companies, Trident also catches its own fish. They have arranged for me to view the fishery up close and personal. And what a difference that makes. If I had never fished with the fishermen and fisherwomen, I wouldn't have learned what I needed to know in order to deliver great tasting fish to our guests. On multiple occasions, Trident allowed me to visit two of its locations in Sand Point and Cordova, Alaska, so I could personally approve the quality and traceability of Trident Seafoods' Wild Alaska Cod and Copper River Coho. I was able to hop aboard fishing boats to fish and see firsthand the entire fishing operation.

Chuck and now his son Joe have always been great partners. They have allowed me to get on the inside of the fishing business so I can fully understand the resource in order to bring phenomenal tasting seafood to our guests. Not only that, they share our values in being responsible stewards for the fishing resource with which we are so blessed.

For as long as Duke Moscrip can remember, fish 'n chips have been one of the most popular things on his menu.

No wonder. This Duke will go to any extreme to get the tastiest fish available.

You can get your Duke's fish 'n chips made with halibut or cod. Accompanied, of course, by hand made French fries that, quite frankly, are darned good.

We think it's great that a restaurant owner, especially a Duke, would go to such extremes to make sure a dish as simple as fish 'n chips would be so special.

Especially dressing up like this just to make the fish look good.

# The Duke of Fish 'n Chips.

# User Friendly
# Fish Tacos &
# Quesadillas

## "Eat Me. I'm Delicious."

# ROCKIN' ROCKFISH TACOS

This is, by far, the biggest flavor bomb on Duke's menu. If you are looking to blow away your guests with juicy flavor, this is it. The combination of the Thai One On Sweet Chili Sauce, Mango Tango Chutney and the sharp white cheddar will have your taste buds dancing.

Makes two tacos

## Ingredients

9 oz Wild Alaska Rockfish fillet

4 Tbsp Thai One On Sweet Chili Sauce (pg 279)

2 Tbsp Let's Be Clarified Butter (pg 148)

2 gordita-style flour tortillas

2 Tbsp Mango Tango Chutney (pg 278)

¼ cup grated Tillamook Extra Sharp cheddar cheese

½ cup Crunchy Slaw Fusion (pg 280)

2 Tbsp grated carrots (optional)

5 cherry tomatoes, halved

6 Tbsp Dukecumber Pico de Gallo (pg 275)

2 Tbsp Tickle Me Tequila Lime Aioli (pg 276)

¼ cup Sultry Salsa (pg 274)

16 Penny's Salsa Corn Tortilla Chips (for scooping)

1 sprig cilantro

## Directions

• Fillet Rockfish using the deep-skin method, which is to remove the gray matter along with the skin. If you are buying from your local fishmonger, ask to have the fillet deep-skinned as well. Be sure to remove all bones.

• Cut into 1½ oz portions (about 3 pieces per taco). Completely submerge in Thai One On Sweet Chili Sauce for 4 hours in the refrigerator.

• Heat a flat griddle or sauté pan to medium-high. Add Let's Be Clarified Butter, and at the same time, sear fish for approximately 4-5 minutes or until fish loses all its translucency, and grill tortillas.

• Smear tortillas with Mango Tango Chutney, and add cheddar until melted.

• Remove from griddle and top with Crunchy Slaw Fusion, tomatoes, shredded carrots and Dukecumber Pico de Gallo. Then drizzle with Tickle Me Tequila Lime Aioli.

• Nestle grilled fish onto tortillas and fold into tacos. Serve with Sultry Salsa and Penny's Salsa Corn Tortilla Chips.

• Garnish with cilantro

# SAILOR BOY SEA COD TACOS

Think of these as the younger, somewhat hotter and more savory version of the Rockin' Rockfish Tacos.

Makes 3 tacos

## Ingredients

9 oz Alaska True Cod fillet

2 tsp Blackening Spice Of Life (pg 323)

2 Tbsp Let's Be Clarified Butter (pg 148)

3 flour tortillas (we use 8-inch, blueberry flour tortillas)

½ cup Crunchy Slaw Fusion (pg 280)

3 Tbsp Tickle Me Tequila Lime Aioli (pg 276)

4 Tbsp crumbled Feta cheese

6 Tbsp Dukecumber Pico de Gallo (pg 275)

½ avocado, diced medium

¼ cup Sultry Salsa (pg 274)

24 Penny's Salsa Corn Tortilla Chips

½ fresh lime

## Directions

- Fillet Cod using the deep-skin method, which is to remove the gray matter along with the skin. If you are buying from your local fishmonger, ask to have the fillet deep-skinned as well. Be sure to remove all bones.

- Cut into 1½-inch square pieces.

- Dust lightly (be careful not to dredge) one side of Cod with Blackening Spice Of Life.

- Melt Let's Be Clarified Butter on a hot flat griddle or sauté pan, and at the same time, grill fish and both sides of the tortillas. Fish is cooked when the internal temperature reaches 130 degrees, approximately 4-5 minutes or until fish has lost all its translucency. Tortillas should be hot but still pliable.

- Stack tortilla with Crunchy Slaw Fusion, Tickle Me Tequila Lime Aioli, the blackened fish, Feta cheese, Dukecumber Pico de Gallo and avocado. Squeeze the juice from half a lime over top of taco, and serve with Sultry Salsa and Penny's Salsa Corn Tortilla Chips.

 Tips from Chef "Wild" Bill:

- Blueberry tortillas are nearly impossible to find, but for a fun family dinner event, try making your own. All you need is a tortilla press, corn flour, lard, salt and fresh blueberries. They are totally unique.

- Instead of making Crunchy Veggie Slaw, you can substitute pre-shredded "Slaw Mix" from the produce section of your local grocery store.

# "ROCK AROUND THE CLOCK" ROCKFISH QUESADILLAS

The best-tasting Rockfish in the world is found in Kodiak, Alaska, where Darius Kasprzak and his fellow fishermen specifically target the species. To most fishermen, Rockfish is a by-catch, which means they ignore this delicate fish until days or weeks later when they bring in their haul. But not Darius and his band of dedicated fishermen. They ice and bleed the fish within minutes of catching them and rush their catch to the Pacific Seafood processing plant in Kodiak. There, experts fillet, vacuum-pack and freeze the fish immediately. Some think it's crazy to say that Darius's frozen Rockfish tastes as good or better than fresh, but it's true. I've tasted Rockfish from every major fishing area, and the combination of great fishermen like Darius and great processing like Pacific Seafood produces the best.

serves three as an appeteaser

## Ingredients

8 oz portion Wild Alaska Rockfish

4 Tbsp Thai One On Sweet Chili Sauce (pg 279)

4 Tbsp Let's Be Clarified Butter (pg 148)

Two 8-inch flour tortillas

½ cup What's Up Wasabi Aioli (pg 321)

2 Tbsp Parmesan cheese and 1 Tbsp Asiago cheese, grated and combined

1 cup Dukecumber Pico de Gallo (pg 275)

pinch fresh organic cilantro, stems removed, diced small

½ cup Sultry Salsa (pg 274)

2 lime wedges

## HAPPY HALIBUT QUESADILLAS

Substitute the Rockfish in the recipe above for a different flavor of this Mexican-inspired dish. We call this little creation the Happy Halibut because it will make you feel good all over. You don't catch Halibut in Mexican waters, but you sure can put it in a Mexican dish; the delicate Halibut flavor mixed with bold cheeses and delicious salsas are a delightful taste sensation.

## Directions

- Fillet Rockfish using the deep-skin method, which is to remove the gray matter along with the skin. If you are buying from your local fishmonger, ask to have the fillet deep-skinned as well. Be sure to remove all bones.

- Cut into 1½-inch square pieces.

- Marinate Rockfish in Thai One On Sweet Chili Sauce for 4 hours in the refrigerator.

- On a hot, flat griddle or sauté pan, sear fish in Let's Be Clarified Butter for 4-5 minutes or until fish has lost all its translucency.

- At the same time, grill one side of the tortillas in Let's Be Clarified Butter. Flip tortilla over and smear with 1 Tbsp What's Up Wasabi Aioli.

- Sprinkle combined cheeses on tortilla. Then top each with ¼ cup Dukecumber Pico de Gallo and spread "coast to coast". Cook tortillas until golden brown and crisp. Distribute grilled Rockfish evenly on tortillas and fold in half. Cut each tortilla into 4 triangles. Top quesadillas with remaining Dukecumber Pico de Gallo and cilantro. Serve with remaining What's Up Wasabi Aioli and Sultry Salsa on the side.

- Squeeze lime wedges to individual taste.

Note from Duke:

The What's Up Wasabi Aioli will blow you away. Once I start eating the aioli, I can't stop. Make extra. I guarantee you'll need it.

# SCINTILLATING SCALLOP TACOS

Jim Stone, one of the owners of the fishing vessel *Provider*, brings in the best Scallops the seas have to offer. They are meaty but succulent, buttery and tender, even when you eat them raw! I begged Jim for over a year to let me come aboard while his crew was fishing so I could see why these are the best Scallops in the world. It's all in the hard work and handling of the Scallops, and his crew is the best. They work twelve-hour shifts, twenty-four hours a day, in rough seas. The Scallops are shelled, sorted, packaged and frozen right on board the ship to lock in that fresh, just-caught flavor that you just can't find anywhere else. Take a look at what I witnessed aboard the *M/V Provider* by looking at our YouTube videos. Type in "Duke Moscrip," and it will take you to all of our videos. The Scallop fishery is simply amazing. I'm honored to serve Jim's Alaska Weathervane Scallops in our tasty taco. They are a perfect twist on this otherwise traditional Mexican recipe.

Makes two tacos

## Ingredients

6 Wild Alaska Weathervane Scallops (size 20 to 30 per lb)

pinch Duke's Ready Anytime Seasoning (pg 323)

2 flour tortillas (we use 8-inch, blueberry flour tortillas (see tip below)

1 Tbsp Let's Be Clarified Butter (pg 148)

½ cup Crunchy Slaw Fusion (pg 280)

3 Tbsp Sinful Citrus Vinaigrette (pg 138)

½ cup Dukecumber Pico de Gallo (pg 275)

2 slices nitrite-free bacon, cooked and chopped into 1-inch pieces

2 Tbsp Tickle Me Tequila Lime Aioli (pg 276)

¼ cup Sultry Salsa (pg 274)

16 Penny's Salsa Corn Tortilla Chips (for scooping)

## Directions

- Season Scallops with Duke's Ready Anytime Seasoning, and sear in olive oil on a hot, flat griddle or sauté pan for approximately 3 minutes per side.

- Grill tortillas in Let's Be Clarified Butter until slightly crisp but still pliable.

- Toss Crunchy Slaw Fusion with Sinful Citrus Vinaigrette and add to tortilla.

- Add Dukecumber Pico de Gallo, bacon and seared Scallops. Drizzle with Tickle Me Tequila Lime Aioli. Serve with Sultry Salsa and Penny's Salsa Corn Tortilla Chips.

 Tip from Chef "Wild" Bill:

Blueberry tortillas are nearly impossible to find, but for a fun family dinner event, try making your own. All you need is a tortilla press, corn flour, lard, salt and fresh blueberries. They are extremely unique.

# Spicy Me Up Sauces & Duke's Coltrane Coleslaw

"For all you spice lovers,
we have the answer."

# SULTRY SALSA gf

Both sensual and spicy, this is a great sauce—flavorful, fresh and unique. You can regulate the amount of heat by increasing or decreasing the amount of Serrano peppers or really turn up the heat by leaving in their seeds. Add to tacos for completely erotic and sensual culinary experience.

**Makes enough for 40 tacos**
(I know; it seems like a lot, but it will keep a while in the refrigerator. It is difficult to make in small batches.)

## Ingredients

2 cups tomatillos, husked

½ cup sweet onions, diced small

1 tsp fresh garlic, diced small

1 serrano pepper, seeds removed, diced small

1 Tbsp fresh organic oregano, stems removed, diced small

½ tsp ground cumin

1 tsp kosher salt

juice from 2 limes

2 cups water

1 avocado, diced small

1 large ripe tomato, diced small

¼ cup fresh cilantro, stems removed, diced small

## Directions

• Place all ingredients in a saucepan and bring to boil. Simmer for about 10 minutes or until tomatillos have softened. Transfer to a shallow pan and cool.

• Purée in a food processor until barely smooth. (Leave a little bit of texture.) This can be made up to 2 days in advance.

• Just before serving, mix in 1 avocado, 1 large ripe tomato and cilantro.

**Note from Duke:**

Penny's makes the best salsa, and they make it for us just like we like it. We have tried to make it ourselves, but, frankly, Penny's makes it better. They also make our coleslaw now, too. I love it when our vendors can do such great work.

# DUKECUMBER PICO DE GALLO gf

This amazing Pico de Gallo was created by our talented Hispanic chefs, boasting bold south of the border flavors in a simple taste treat.

Makes enough for 12 tacos

## Ingredients

1 cup ripe tomato, diced

¼ cup green onions, green parts only, diced small

1 cup cucumber, peeled, seeds removed and diced small

½ tsp crushed red pepper

juice from 1 lemon

½ tsp kosher salt

¼ bunch cilantro, stems removed, diced medium

## Directions

• Mix well and refrigerate.

 Tip from Chef "Wild" Bill:

Serve this with chips and salsa, or use it as a topping for broiled chicken breast or as a great filling for your cheese quesadilla. It adds crunch and flavor to almost any salad and is also good served as a tostada. Try adding chopped fresh avocado and garnish with cilantro sprigs.

# The Sauce That Makes You Want To Salsa Dance

The first time I tried Penny's tortilla chips, I was in disbelief. How could they be this good! I had been disappointed all my life with tortilla chips. Too moist, too crunchy, too hard, too mealy, too thin, too thick, too soft, goes stale too fast. I am a tortilla snob and hard to please. They continue to be consistently the best chip I have ever tasted. And their salsa is

incredible, as is their coleslaw. Since 1995, Duke's has had a relationship with this local Northwest company based in Auburn, WA. Owner Ryan Hershey just knows how to make the tastiest Mexican food north of the border.

# GUADALAJARA GUACAMOLE gf

Guac so good you could eat it with a spoon—I often do. This is excellent with ceviche and pretty much any other seafood or just the way that guacamole was made famous . . . on a Penny's Salsa Corn Tortilla Chip.

Makes one appeteaser serving for two

## Ingredients

1 perfectly ripe avocado

¼ cup Dukecumber Pico de Gallo (pg 275)

## Directions

- In a mixing bowl, smash avocado with a fork. Then combine with Dukecumber Pico de Gallo.


# TICKLE ME TEQUILA LIME AIOLI gf

. . . and that's just what it will do, tickle your taste buds with flavor.

Makes 22 Tbsp (enough for about 11 Scintillating Scallop Tacos)

## Ingredients

1 cup Make It Yourself Mayo (pg 320) or buy one made with olive oil

¼ cup fresh squeezed lime juice

½ tsp kosher salt

½ tsp black pepper

½ tsp fresh organic parsley, stems removed, diced small

1 Tbsp fresh garlic, diced small

1 Tbsp tequila

## Directions

- Mix all ingredients together in mixing bowl.

# MANGO TANGO CHUTNEY gf

A sauce that may literally have you dancing when you add it to your tacos; it blends all kinds of flavors you would never think to combine. Just like the tango, there are few rules and a million variations that make this dressing dance.

**Makes 4 cups** (enough for about 33 Rockin' Rockfish Tacos). This is another recipe that is difficult to make in small batches. Just invite more people for dinner!

## Ingredients

3 Tbsp extra virgin olive oil

1 large Walla Walla Sweet onion, diced medium

1 sweet red pepper, diced medium

¼ cup ginger root, peeled and minced

1 tsp crushed red pepper flakes

4 ripe (slightly soft) mangos, flesh extracted and sliced

1 cup pineapple juice

½ cup cider vinegar

½ cup sugar in the raw

2 Tbsp yellow curry powder

pinch kosher salt

pinch white pepper

## Directions

- Heat olive oil on medium heat and add onions, peppers, ginger and pepper flakes. Cook until soft.

- Add remaining ingredients and stir until sugar and spices are dissolved.

- Bring to boil, stirring continuously. Then reduce heat and simmer for 10 minutes or to desired thickness.

 Tips from Chef "Wild" Bill:

- You can get crazy with variations here! Add pecans, almonds or macadamias. Or fruit, raisins, dried cranberries or dried cherries. However, for fish tacos, I keep it simple; there is a ton of flavor already there.

- If you are crunched for time, Major Grey's Mango Chutney (found in most grocery stores) is pretty good, but fresh from your own kitchen is definitely better.

# THAI ONE ON SWEET CHILI SAUCE gf

Combining the sweet, salty and spicy flavors made famous in Thailand, this chili sauce is great for marinating seafood or dipping anything that craves a sweet and spicy accompaniment.

Makes 2 cups of sauce

## Ingredients

1 cup honey (local, sustainable and organic)

1 cup Sweet Thai Chili Sauce (see below)

## Directions

- Mix and store at room temperature.

 Tip from Chef "Wild" Bill:

This is a simple but tasty dip for Coconut Prawns. It's also great with Egg Rolls or Spring Rolls.


# SWEET THAI CHILI SAUCE gf

This is the foundation for the Thai One On Sweet Chili Sauce. Less sweet, but you'll notice it is much more pungent and powerful.

Makes 2 cups of sauce

## Ingredients

1 cup cold water

2 tsp cornstarch

1 cup rice vinegar

¼ cup sugar in the raw

2 tsp fresh ginger root, peeled and minced

2 tsp fresh garlic, diced small

2 tsp hot chili pepper (jalapeno, serrano or Thai), minced

3 tsp Organic or All Natural Heinz Ketchup (make your own or purchase one with no high fructose corn syrup)

 Tip from Chef "Wild" Bill:

A decent shortcut is to buy Mae Ploy Sweet Chili Sauce, found in most grocery stores.

## Directions

- Stir cornstarch and water until dissolved; let sit, then stir again.

- In a heavy-gauge saucepan, bring vinegar and sugar to a boil.

- Add ginger, garlic, chili pepper and ketchup, and let simmer for 5 minutes.

- Add water/corn starch mixture and heat until just boiling.

- Cool in refrigerator. After cooling, you can thin the sauce if necessary by whisking in a little water. Keep refrigerated.

# DUKE'S COLTRANE COLESLAW gf

Just like the brilliant jazz musician John Coltrane, a good coleslaw delivers notes of sweetness that keep you yearning for more.

*Serves four as a side dish*

## Ingredients

1 cup Crunchy Slaw Fusion

1 oz Duke's Coltrane Coleslaw Dressing

### Crunchy Slaw Fusion

1 lb green and red cabbage, diced small

½ lb Napa cabbage, diced small

½ bunch fresh cilantro, stems removed, diced small

¼ lb snap peas, julienned sliced

### Duke's Coltrane Coleslaw Dressing

1 organic egg

¼ cup organic cane sugar

1 Tbsp fresh garlic, diced small

1 Tbsp fresh ginger, diced small

1 tsp Lea & Perrins Worcestershire Sauce

6 Tbsp dried mission figs, diced small

1 Tbsp soy sauce (we use San-J Tamari Gluten-Free Soy Sauce)

¾ cup GMO-free canola oil

¼ cup sesame oil

6 Tbsp rice wine vinegar

6 Tbsp pineapple juice

¼ cup green onions, green parts only, minced

2 Tbsp white sesame seeds

2 Tbsp black sesame seeds

## Directions

- Just before serving, toss Duke's Coltrane Coleslaw Dressing with Crunchy Slaw Fusion. This will keep it crunchy and fresh.

- Mix all ingredients and refrigerate in a covered container.

- Add egg to a mixer and froth with whisk attachment. Add sugar, garlic, ginger and Lea & Perrins, and mix until sugar is completely dissolved.

- Purée soy sauce and dried figs together in a food processor, about 2-3 minutes. Add to egg mixture.

- In a separate bowl, combine canola and sesame oil. In a slow, steady stream, add to egg mixture until emulsified.

- Add vinegar and pineapple juice, then green onions and sesame seeds.

- Store covered in the refrigerator.

# Finger Lickin' Good...

Ribs,
Chicken,
Burgers,
& Steak

# SOON TO BE SOLD OUT BBQ RIBS

I always loved the ribs at El Gaucho, one of my favorite Seattle restaurants. I always dreamed of making them myself. Fortunately, I was invited to El Gaucho's kitchen and observed their preparation. I realized that there was another great way to do them—a little differently from El Gaucho but just as tasty.

Serves two very hungry people

## Ingredients

2 racks baby back pork ribs

1¼ cups Chef "Wild" Bill's Barbecue Sauce (pg 287)

¼ cup Sold Out Rib Rub (pg 286)

bacon fat reserved from preparing Chef "Wild" Bill's Barbecue Sauce

liquid smoke (we use Wright's All Natural)

½ cup Walla Walla Sweet Haystack Onion Straws (pg 286)

 Tip from Chef "Wild" Bill:
Plan for a full and glorious day of cooking. These babies take time, but they are worth the effort.

## Directions

• Preheat oven to 450 degrees.

• Remove the "silver" from the back of the ribs by running a fork down one of the bones; then grab the membrane and peel. This is the first step to tender ribs.

• Lightly baste the ribs with reserved bacon fat from the barbecue sauce and season liberally with Sold Out Rib Rub.

• On a hot grill, mark ribs just long enough to make visible grill marks. In a quarter-sized hotel pan (approximately 20 inch by 10 inch), add ½ gallon of water and ¼ cup natural liquid smoke, and stack a perforated 4-inch pan over it. Place ribs on the perforated pan and make a foil tent (no holes) over them. This will steam/bake them and keep them moist.

• Bake in preheated 450 degree oven for approximately 3 hours. (Bake time varies depending on size of ribs.) Test for doneness by bending the ribs backwards; they should begin to tear apart easily and be very tender but not overly soft. If ribs need more baking time, make sure to recreate the airtight seal with the foil so they continue to steam.

• Remove from the oven and brush each rack with 6 Tbsp Chef "Wild" Bill's Barbecue Sauce.

• Return to the oven until sauce is very hot (180 degrees), approximately 6 minutes.

• Serve with Walla Walla Sweet Haystack Onion Straws.

# SOLD OUT RIB RUB

## Ingredients

1 cup sugar

1 cup salt

½ cup Blackening Spice Of Life (pg 323)

½ cup granulated garlic

½ cup organic dry thyme

½ cup organic dry marjoram

¼ cup paprika

¼ cup white pepper

2 Tbsp cayenne pepper

1½ Tbsp organic dry oregano

1½ Tbsp organic dry basil

1½ Tbsp organic dry rosemary

## Directions

• Combine and store in an airtight container.

# WALLA WALLA SWEET HAYSTACK ONION STRAWS

There is nothing quite like the sweet and savory smell and taste of a Walla Walla Sweet onion. When you dress them up like we do, they are amazing on their own, or they can add a little crunch and personality to BBQ ribs or your favorite sandwich or burger.

**Makes approximately 16 servings**

## Ingredients

2 cups Walla Walla Sweet onions, sliced paper-thin

¼ cup Darigold buttermilk

2 cups Baja Bandito Flour (pg 330)

GMO-free canola oil for frying

## Directions

• Combine onions with buttermilk and refrigerate for about 15 minutes.

• Pour enough oil into a heavy-gauge saucepan to submerge onions completely. Heat to 325-350 degrees. (Use a candy thermometer and adjust oil slowly.)

• Drain excess buttermilk from onions; then toss in Baja Bandito Flour until lightly dusted.

• Tap dusted rings to remove excess flour, and fry until golden brown and crisp.

# CHEF "WILD" BILL'S BARBECUE SAUCE

## Ingredients

2 strips nitrite-free bacon

¼ cup sweet onions, diced small

3 cups Organic or All Natural Heinz Ketchup
(make your own or purchase one with no high
fructose corn syrup)

¼ cup brown sugar

1 Tbsp dry mustard (we use Colman's)

½ cup brewed regular coffee

1 Tbsp white wine vinegar

2 Tbsp soy sauce (we use San-J Gluten-Free Tamari
Soy Sauce)

2 Tbsp Lea & Perrins Worcestershire Sauce

¼ tsp crushed red pepper (if you like spice, try ½ tsp)

½ cup molasses

5 Tbsp plum sauce (available in most grocery stores)

1 Tbsp liquid smoke (we use Wright's All Natural)

2 Tbsp honey (local, sustainable and organic)

## Directions

• Cut raw bacon into 1-inch pieces and render in a heavy-gauge roasting pan until nearly done.

• Add sweet onions and cook until bacon is done and onions are soft.

• Reserve excess bacon fat for rubbing ribs before cooking.

• Add all remaining ingredients, and cook at 165 degrees until liquid is nearly black and thick, around 6 hours. Strain sauce through a fine sieve and refrigerate.

## Tip from Chef "Wild" Bill:

Serve with moistened, heated towels.
These ribs are messy!

# "SCREAMING GOOD" GRILLED CHICKEN SANDWICH

Free range, all natural, no antibiotics, just chickens allowed to be chickens.

Serves one

## Ingredients

6 oz Harvestland/Perdue chicken breast

¼ avocado, sliced

2 slices nitrite-free bacon

2 Tbsp Make It Yourself Mayo (pg 320)

1 slice Jarlsberg Swiss cheese

1 slice Tillamook Extra Sharp cheddar cheese

2 Tbsp Let's Be Clarified Butter (pg 148)

2 slices tomato

¼ cup iceberg lettuce, shredded

2 slices Essential Baking Company Rosemary Bread

3 Tbsp Chef "Wild" Bill's Barbecue Sauce (pg 287)

1 tsp Duke's Ready Anytime Seasoning (pg 323)

## Directions

- Slice chicken breast in half horizontally.

- Place ½ breasts on broiler. Cook until translucency disappears but make sure the internal temperature is at least 165 degrees for good food handling practices, approximately 4-5 minutes per side.

- While chicken is cooking, heat Let's Be Clarified Butter on grill. Place rosemary bread on top of butter and grill until crisp.

- Spread Make It Yourself Mayo on bread "coast to coast".

- Top chicken with Tillamook Extra Sharp Cheddar and Jarlsberg Swiss. Add bacon on top and place in cheese melter or under broiler until cheese is melted and bacon is hot.

- Add shredded iceberg lettuce, tomatoes and avocado. Slice in half diagonally.

# Chickens Allowed To Be Chickens

It's not easy finding all natural, cage-free chickens that are frozen properly. Why frozen, you ask? Because, if frozen correctly and quickly, they are consistently better tasting than fresh. Fresh takes several days to get to the restaurant, losing valuable freshness. In fact, the transportation challenges can result in chickens that are seven days old. That's too old for me and our guests. Properly frozen chicken wins every time because it captures the freshness every time.

Here's an emphatic note from Natalie Gilley of Harvestland/Perdue: "NO ANTIBIOTICS. NO EXCEPTIONS. At Harvestland/Perdue, everything we do is about great tasting food. When we say, 'No antibiotics ever' chicken, we mean it. No exceptions and no fine print. Also, all-vegetarian diet, no animal by-products, no hormones or steroids."

Just chickens allowed to be chickens.

# Best Quality Ingredients Leads To The Best Guest Experience

If you want to have great food, you need people who can help you find it, people who will get off their tails and help you source the best ingredients. It requires people who will think outside the box, dig a little deeper, and make some phone calls. You need great purveyors to have great tasting food. One of the reasons we have had great success with our food is that we have Food Services of America to help us. When I call Greg Gearhart or Alan Caraco at FSA and ask them to research a new product, they are all over it. They understand our concept and what we are trying to do—bring our guests the best, all-natural, chemical-free, preservative-free products. Our partnership with FSA spans decades because it believes in partnering with us to do what we want, not what it has to offer us. FSA is a big company with systems and procedures, and its employees understand how to get things done within their parameters. It takes a commitment of the whole company to deliver what we want. FSA is that kind of purveyor.

## Grass-Fed Beef Is The Best

When we asked the staff at FSA to help us source grass-fed beef, they had the answer. We had been trying to work with local grass-fed providers, but they just could not deliver a product in volume, on time, and consistently. We often did not trust that the product was truly grass-fed and healthy. FSA introduced us to its own meat company, Ameristar Meats, operated by Tim Loveall, a custom meat cutting and processing company. It researched grass-fed beef and our connection with Australia began to materialize. We came to realize that Australia has the best track record and best processing of grass-fed beef in the world. It has never had an outbreak of E. coli in its entire history. The U.S. gets as many as five incidents per year. Without Ameristar, we might never have been able to find such an incredible source. The taste is right, the health is right, and the safety is outstanding.

Some people might think it's strange that a Chowder House would serve a great cheeseburger. Not Duke Moscrip. He knows that man cannot live by chowder alone.

The great tasting cheeseburger now served at all four Duke's Chowder House locations is almost the same sandwich that Duke cooked up in the seventies when he opened his first restaurant on Queen Anne. Except for the bun.

"A great burger's gotta have a great bun," Duke proudly states. "And I searched everywhere for the best bun I could find." Several years ago he found it, and his cheeseburger was better than ever.

Now you can always find Duke's classic cheeseburger on the menu, along with eight different chowders, lotsa seafood items, crispy fish 'n chips, Duke's signature Caesar salad, and some other great burgers, like chicken, salmon, blackened halibut and tuna.

It may say Chowder House on the door. But it's really a great place to eat all of your favorite things.

# The Duke of Sandwich.

# NORTH OF CALIFORNIA BURGER

First we go Southwest to Australia, then Northwest to Duke's for the best burger in the world. It's a unique combination and one you'll only see Southwest and then . . . North Of California.

Serves one

## Ingredients

7 oz ground beef (grass-fed Australian preferred)

½ tsp Duke's Ready Anytime Seasoning (pg 323)

1 burger bun (we use Essential Baking Company Nearly Brioche Burger Bun)

1 Tbsp Let's Be Clarified Butter (pg 148)

2 slices Jarlsberg Swiss cheese

2 slices nitrite-free bacon, cooked

¼ fresh avocado, sliced and fanned

2 Tbsp Hold Me Tight Chipotle Aioli (pg 322)

¼ cup iceberg lettuce, finely shredded

2 tomato slices

¼ cup Walla Walla Sweet Haystack Onion Straws (pg 286)

## Directions

- Shape burger into a round and sprinkle with Duke's Ready Anytime Seasoning.

- Broil burger to desired doneness, but make sure the internal temperature is at least 165 degrees for good food handling practices, approximately 4-5 minutes per side.

- While burger cooks, grill the Nearly Brioche Burger Bun in Let's Be Clarified Butter until almost finished; then place both slices of Jarlsberg Swiss cheese on the top bun and melt under broiler. (Be careful not to melt too much.)

- Add bacon and avocado and spread bottom bun with Hold Me Tight Chipotle Aioli.

- Add shredded lettuce, tomatoes and Walla Walla Sweet Haystack Onion Straws.

- Add burger to bottom bun.

- Serve with Fish Or Cut Bait French Fries and Organic or All Natural Heinz Ketchup.

 Tip from Chef "Wild" Bill:

For a gluten-free burger bun, try Shambala Bakery located on Camano Island, WA. Canadian brand Kinnikinnick also makes a good one.

# Making Cheese The Old Fashioned Way . . . Naturally

What is impressive to me about Tillamook is that the cheese is made naturally, unlike many cheeses in the marketplace. There is no attempt to speed things up with chemicals in order to shorten the period of time that the cheese is aging.

Tillamook's cheese recipe and natural aging process hasn't changed in more than 100 years and makes all the difference in flavor and quality. Tillamook is all about consistency, tradition and patience… very much like Duke's Chowder House. They naturally age their cheddar cheeses a minimum of sixty days and up to five years to develop a richer, sharper and deeper flavor. Their natural cheese is made without any preservatives, artificial ingredients, and is rBST hormone free—it's 100 percent real cheese—and has won more than 700 awards since 1904 including World's Best Medium Cheddar Cheese and World's Best Colby Jack Cheese at the World Championship Cheese Contest.

# Tillamook®

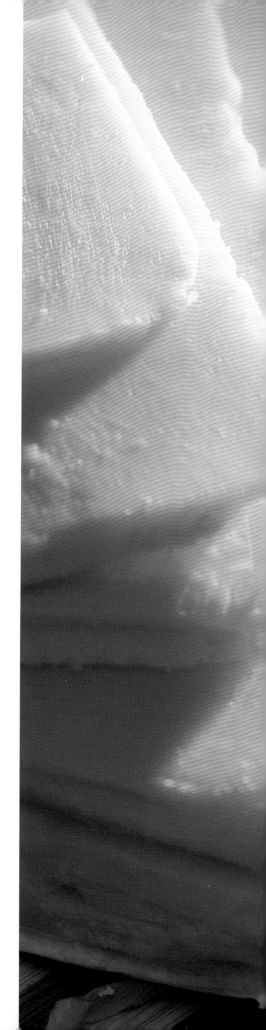

# DUKE'S "EXTRA SHARP" CHEDDAR CHEESEBURGER

We have always used Tillamook "Extra Sharp" cheddar cheese. "Extra Sharp" cheddar makes the difference between an average burger and a great one, and Tillamook makes the best. Unlike a lot of cheese makers, Tillamook uses a natural method to age its cheese and get the taste just right. There are no chemicals in anything Tillamook does. It takes a little longer to make cheese this way but at Duke's, we don't mind waiting. It just wouldn't be a Duke's cheeseburger without Tillamook Extra Sharp White Cheddar.

Serves one

## Ingredients

7 oz ground beef (grass-fed Australian preferred)

½ tsp Duke's Ready Anytime Seasoning (pg 323)

1 burger bun (we use Essential Baking Company Nearly Brioche Burger Bun)

1 Tbsp Let's Be Clarified Butter (pg 148)

2 slices Tillamook Extra Sharp cheddar cheese

2 Tbsp Make It Yourself Mayo (pg 320) or buy one made with olive oil

¼ cup iceberg lettuce, finely shredded

2 tomato slices

¼ cup Walla Walla Sweet Haystack Onion Straws (pg 286)

20 Fish Or Cut Bait French Fries (pg 259)

Organic or All Natural Heinz Ketchup (make your own or purchase one with no high fructose corn syrup) for dipping

 Tip from Chef "Wild" Bill:
For a gluten-free burger bun, try Shambala Bakery located on Camano Island, WA. Canadian brand Kinnikinnick also makes a good one.

## Directions

- Shape burger into a round and sprinkle with Duke's Ready Anytime Seasoning.

- Broil burger to desired doneness. Make sure the internal temperature is at least 165 degrees for good food handling practices, approximately 4-5 minutes per side.

- While burger cooks, grill the Nearly Brioche Burger Bun in Let's Be Clarified Butter until almost finished; then place both slices of cheese on the top bun and melt under broiler. (Be careful not to melt too much.)

- Spread top bun with Make It Yourself Mayo.

- Add shredded lettuce, tomatoes and Walla Walla Sweet Haystack Onion Straws.

- Add burger to bottom bun.

- Serve with Fish Or Cut Bait French Fries and Organic or All Natural Heinz Ketchup.

### Note from Duke:

Some guests have asked me, "Why do you have burgers at a Seafood Restaurant? Here's what I say. You can't eat Seafood every night. We have sourced, arguably, the best burger in the world. Our beef is all grass-fed from Australia, and the Nearly Brioche Burger Bun was perfected by our bakers at Essential Baking Company. Trust me; one bite and you will be saying, "It's sooo good."

# Fries For Forever

The "chips" part of the Fish & Chips is extremely important to those who love the dish. Lousy fries and you can say goodbye to those folks. Don't get me wrong, fish is the most important, but lousy fries just won't cut it. Simplot makes our fries nice and plump with plenty of potato flavor and custom-made spices. Crispy, crunchy, and ready for Heinz Ketchup or Duke's "Give Me More Tartar Sauce."

I have been to Boise and toured the French fry plant. There's a reason Jack Simplot built an empire. He literally invented French fries and his company continues to make the best.

# They Make It Better Than We Do

Can you imagine having French fries without ketchup? It would seem Un-American. But not just any ketchup. To pass Duke's strict standards, it has to be natural with no chemicals and no preservatives. Heinz qualifies on all counts. In fact, "Wild" Bill and I tried to make ketchup ourselves a while back when looking for a natural product. Fortunately, Heinz came to the rescue with its all natural, silky smooth, fresh tomatoey taste. We could not make it as good as Heinz. What a product!

It's hard to believe, but did you know that Heinz has been making its savory tangy Ketchup since 1876? Honest and pure products were what Henry Heinz was making, and he wanted everyone to see that, so he used clear glass bottles with the keystone label as the company was founded in Pennsylvania, the keystone state. And did you know that Heinz sends out more than 6 billion seeds each year to farmers who grow tomatoes specifically for Heinz?

Henry J. Heinz believed, "To do a common thing uncommonly well brings success." We at Duke's certainly share his belief.

# "FOOL AROUND & FALL IN LOVE" FILET MIGNON ...DUKE'S WAY gf

What can I say? I'm a bleu cheese dressing addict.

Serves one

## Ingredients

8 oz grass-fed beef filet

1 tsp Duke's Ready Anytime Seasoning (pg 323)

1 tsp black peppercorns, coarse grind

½ cup Nothing But Blue Sky Bleu Cheese Dressing (pg 139)

## Directions

• Sprinkle Duke's Ready Anytime Seasoning on top and bottom of filet.

• Roll side of steak in pepper all the way around steak, pressing firmly to ensure that peppercorns adhere.

• Broil filet, approximately 5 minutes per side, depending on desired doneness.

• Pour puddle of Nothing But Blue Sky Bleu Cheese Dressing on plate.

• Place filet on top of dressing.

# Not So Serious Side Dishes

Have fun with your food,
take yourself lightly and
enjoy your guests.

# BABY I LOVE YOU RED POTATOES &
# IT'S THE REAL THING FINGERLING POTATOES gf

Potatoes are the perfect complement to meaty fish—and meaty meat for that matter. The most important potato point I can make is to keep it simple. Don't overdo or overthink potatoes. They just need a little company to pull out the impressive flavors they naturally provide.

Serves 4

## Ingredients

10 medium organic baby red potatoes or organic fingerling potatoes

½ tsp Duke's Ready Anytime Seasoning (pg 323)

½ cup + 2 Tbsp extra virgin olive oil

½ tsp fresh garlic, diced small

½ tsp Duke's Superb Herb Blend (pg 322)

4 1-inch coins Compound Tasty Herb Butter (pg 147)

## Directions

• Boil enough lightly salted water to cover potatoes completely and blanch until al dente or "firm to the bite," but not hard (about 25 minutes).

• Shock with ice water until completely cool. Cut potatoes in half.

• Preheat oven to 400.

• In a baking pan, toss potatoes in olive oil and Duke's Ready Anytime Seasoning.

• Roast at 400 degrees until light golden brown (about 15 minutes).

• Toss potatoes with garlic and Duke's Superb Herb Blend and top with Compound Tasty Herb Butter.

# ONE POTATO TWO POTATO PANCAKES

Potato Pancakes have long been a tradition of European and Middle Eastern Cultures. The Northwest is the heart of potato country, so we had to bring this tradition to Duke's. With our unique blend of flavors and spices, these little beauties are an amazing complement to any main dish. My son John is crazy for these. And, it's all about balance with a little bit of charm and elegance to keep the taste buds intrigued and wanting more.

Makes approximately 20 pancakes

## Ingredients

3 lbs organic Yukon Gold potatoes, cut into quarters

½ cup heavy whipping cream

12 Roasted Garlic Cloves (pg 328)

2 Tbsp Duke's Ready Anytime Seasoning (pg 323)

2 Tbsp Duke's Superb Herb Blend (pg 322)

1½ cups grated Asiago cheese

2 Tbsp Darigold butter

¼ cup horseradish purée

2 cups panko breadcrumbs (available at most grocery stores)

2 Tbsp Let's Be Clarified Butter (pg 148)

## Directions

• Boil enough lightly salted water to cover potatoes completely and boil until soft (about 25 minutes).

• Drain in a colander until all excess moisture is removed. Place in a dry pan and set aside.

• In a food processor, blend all ingredients except potatoes, panko and Let's Be Clarified Butter.

• Using a hand-mixer, blend (or mash by hand) all ingredients, including potatoes. Place in a shallow pan and chill in the refrigerator for at least 2 hours.

• Pat mixture into small snowballs, roll lightly in panko, and then flatten.

• On a flat griddle or sauté pan, grill potato pancakes in Let's Be Clarified Butter for 2-3 minutes or until golden brown.

# LET'S GET SMASHED POTATOES gf

Serve along with a few shots of whiskey and your potatoes won't be the only thing at the table that's "smashed." Just kidding; we all know how much is too much, right? The key to the delicate crunch of these perfectly smashed potatoes is beautifully browned Asiago cheese that will make you think you've never had too much.

**Makes approximately 20 portions**

## Ingredients

3 lbs organic Yukon Gold potatoes, cut into quarters

½ cup heavy whipping cream

12 Roasted Garlic Cloves (pg 328)

2 Tbsp Duke's Ready Anytime Seasoning (pg 323)

2 Tbsp Duke's Superb Herb Blend (pg 322)

1½ cups grated Asiago cheese

2 Tbsp Darigold butter

## Directions

• Boil enough lightly salted water to cover potatoes completely and boil until soft (about 25 minutes).

• Drain in a colander until all excess moisture is removed. Place in a dry pan and set aside.

• In a food processor, blend all ingredients except potatoes, reserving a small amount of roasted garlic, cheese and Duke's Superb Herb Blend for garnish.

• Using a hand-mixer, beat blended ingredients into the potatoes.

# SNAP TO ATTENTION PEAS gf

Snap peas are always ready for action. They don't require close attention like other vegetables—for instance, broccoli, which can go limp pretty quickly if overcooked even a little. The sweet taste and crispy texture of these peas will definitely hold your attention long after they're gone.

Makes 6 servings

## Ingredients

¼ cup extra virgin olive oil

2 Tbsp fresh garlic, diced small

½ cup tomatoes, diced

1 lb snap peas, no blemishes, washed and stems removed (tip below)

½ tsp Duke's Ready Anytime Seasoning (pg 323)

## Directions

• In a large sauté pan, heat olive oil on high but do not smoke.

• Add garlic and sauté for about 30 seconds but do not brown.

• Add tomatoes and sauté for 1 minute.

• Add snap peas and heat until just hot—they should still be crunchy.

 Tips from Chef "Wild" Bill:

• Try them as a snack. Snap peas are a favorite around my house. We snack on them right out of the garden. My kids love them. The key is to barely cook them.

• To remove stems, gently pull backwards and the string will pull off at the same time. The strings are tough and very hard to digest. If you simply cut off the stems, the strings will remain attached.

# SHUCK AND JIVE CORN ON THE COB gf

This summertime favorite with lots of butter and sea salt makes me wish we had corn on the cob all year round. But there is something about the warm summer weather that adds to the magic of corn on the cob. It always tastes just a bit sweeter when the summer sun is shining in your face with every buttery bite.

Makes 4 servings of corn

## Ingredients

4 ears of really fresh, fresh, fresh corn, shucked and cleaned

pinch Duke's Ready Anytime Seasoning (pg 323) or sea salt

4 Tbsp Darigold butter

## Directions

- Place corn on broil grates of barbecue and close the lid. This will steam and broil them at the same time.

- Rotate a quarter turn as soon as corn begins to darken until the whole ear is cooked.

- Roll in butter and dust with Duke's Ready Anytime Seasoning or sea salt.

# SPARE ME ASPARAGUS gf

. . . or rather, don't. Asparagus is delicious and has the most amazing texture of just about any vegetable. When combined with our Duke's Ready Anytime Seasoning, the flavors that come out of these spears will make you say, "Hello, Asparagus; where have you been all my life?"

Makes one serving

## Ingredients

7 fresh asparagus spears

1 tsp extra virgin olive oil

½ tsp fresh garlic, diced small

1 tsp Duke's Ready Anytime Seasoning (pg 323)

## Directions

- Remove all white sections of the asparagus stalks.

- Rub with extra virgin olive oil and garlic. Toss with Duke's Ready Anytime Seasoning.

- Place asparagus spears on the barbecue, giving them grill marks, which will give them a smoky taste. Transfer to a sauté pan and cook until they are al dente. They should be nice and crisp.

 Tip from Chef "Wild" Bill:

If you are having a large party and need more BBQ space, after marking the asparagus spears on the grill, sauté them only briefly, about 1 minute; then put them on a sheet pan with a little more olive oil. When you're ready for dinner, bake on the sheet pan until hot, leaving asparagus crisp.

# SQUASH ME AND ZUCCHINI ME gf

Washington State is home to the best organic squash and zucchini in the world. These often overlooked vegetables pull flavors from any herbs and spices you might add, and that can make them spectacular.

Makes 8 servings

## Ingredients

1 large organic zucchini, cut in half lengthwise, then sliced into chunks at an angle

1 large organic yellow squash, cut in half lengthwise, then sliced into chunks at an angle

2 Tbsp extra virgin olive oil

1 Tbsp fresh organic herbs (basil, oregano, thyme, rosemary, stems removed from each), minced and blended together

14 grains of sea salt (try Hawaiian pink—it's beautiful)

pinch Duke's Ready Anytime Seasoning (pg 323)

## Directions

- In a sauté pan, heat olive oil to hot; then add zucchini and yellow squash, and sauté until golden brown. (Be careful not to over-cook; squash should be firm but not hard).

- Add herbs, cook for 1 minute, then add Duke's Ready Anytime Seasoning. Serve and sprinkle with sea salt.

 Tip from Chef "Wild" Bill:

Cutting zucchini and squash in large chunks helps prevent over-cooking.

# Scrumptious Sauces & Savory Seasonings

"I continue to say,
It's really all about
the condiments."

# BASIL ALMOND PRETTY PESTO gf

Traditional pesto is made with pine nuts, which are delicious but very expensive, and if they aren't roasted right, they can be a little "off" tasting. Chef "Wild" Bill converted me to this pesto made without pine nuts. The almonds are fantastic and one of the healthiest foods on Duke's menu.

**Makes enough for 10 portions Wild Alaska Salmon With Pretty Pesto**

## Ingredients

1 cup fresh organic basil (tightly packed)

¼ cup Roasted Garlic Cloves (pg 328)

¼ cup roasted almonds

¼ cup Parmesan cheese and ¼ cup Asiago cheese, grated and combined

1 Tbsp Duke's Ready Anytime Seasoning (pg 323)

2 Tbsp fresh lemon juice

5 oz or 10 Tbsp extra virgin olive oil

## Directions

• Blend all ingredients except olive oil in a food processor. Slowly add olive oil until emulsified. Keep refrigerated.

# MAKE IT YOURSELF MAYO gf

Simple to make and better than store-bought, it's the mother of all sauces and the base for many as well. I don't think I could live without mayonnaise—it goes with just about everything. True confession, I even eat it with peanut butter.

**Makes approximately 1 cup**

## Ingredients

1 large egg yolk or 1½ Tbsp pasteurized organic egg yolks

1 tsp fresh lemon juice

1 tsp white wine vinegar

pinch salt

½ cup olive oil

½ cup GMO-free canola oil

## Directions

• Place the egg yolk in a food processor and beat on high until frothy, about 2 minutes.

• Add lemon juice, white wine vinegar and salt and beat for another minute.

• While the blades are running, very slowly add oils in a very thin stream. If you add too fast, the mayonnaise will not emulsify. Cover and refrigerate.

 Tip from Chef "Wild" Bill:

Liven up your mayo by adding a garlic clove during the first step to make a garlic mayo. Or add a tablespoon of honey and Dijon mustard to make a honey mustard mayo. Pick some basil or tarragon from your garden to make an herb mayo. The possibilities are endless.

# WHAT'S UP WASABI AIOLI gf

A little spice to singe the nostrils just a bit. This stuff is addicting.

Makes approximately 1 cup

## Ingredients

1½ cup Make It Yourself Mayo (pg 320) or buy one made with olive oil

1 Tbsp rice vinegar (we use Aji Marin)

1 tsp fresh ginger, peeled and minced

1 Tbsp soy sauce (we use San-J Gluten-Free Tamari Soy Sauce)

1 tsp sugar

2 Tbsp wasabi powder

3 Tbsp fresh organic parsley, stems removed, diced small

## Directions

• Blend all ingredients until dissolved and well-mixed.

# ZESTY LUSTY LIME AIOLI gf

This punches up the flavor of more subtle seafood like Rockfish or Cod. It's also excellent with sautéed or poached Prawns.

Makes approximately 3 cups

## Ingredients

3 fresh garlic cloves

1 cup Hold Me Tight Chipotle Aioli (pg 322)

1 cup Make It Yourself Mayo (pg 320) or buy one made with olive oil

½ cup Sweet Thai Chili Sauce (pg 279)

juice from 2 fresh limes

1 Tbsp Duke's Superb Herb Blend (pg 322)

1 Tbsp fresh organic parsley

pinch crushed red pepper flakes

pinch Duke's Ready Anytime Seasoning

## Directions

• Process garlic in a food processor; then add remaining ingredients and blend until smooth. Cover and refrigerate.

# HOLD ME TIGHT CHIPOTLE AIOLI gf

Smokey and sweet, this delicious aioli is a complement to anything seafood, especially Salmon.

Makes approximately 2¾ cups

### Ingredients

2 cups Make It Yourself Mayo (pg 320) or buy one made with olive oil

¼ cup honey (local, sustainable and organic)

¼ cup stone-ground mustard

3½ Tbsp chipotle purée (purée a small can of chipotle peppers and keep in an air-tight container in your refrigerator)

### Directions

• Purée ingredients and store covered in the refrigerator.


# DUKE'S SUPERB HERB BLEND gf

These herbs make everything taste great.

Makes approximately 1 cup

### Ingredients

½ cup fresh organic rosemary, stems removed, diced small
½ cup fresh organic thyme, stems removed, diced small
½ cup fresh organic oregano, stems removed, diced small

### Directions

• Mix all ingredients and store in an airtight container.


# BALSAMIC SOY REDUCTION SAUCE gf

Makes ¼ cup

### Ingredients

½ cup high-quality balsamic vinegar

½ cup soy sauce (we use San-J Gluten-Free Tamari Soy Sauce)

 Tip from Chef "Wild" Bill:
Be careful not to over-reduce and burn this (which will make a big mess of your pot).

### Directions

• In a heavy-gauge saucepan, bring soy and balsamic vinegar to a boil and continue cooking, stirring occasionally, until the liquid thickens to a syrup-like consistency. Set aside.

# DUKE'S READY ANYTIME SEASONING gf

This is your go-to spice for French fries or anything broiled. It's perfect for mixing up in a big batch and storing for use "anytime." It's savory and salty with a little heat, and herbs to mellow out the burn.

Makes approximately 3 cups

## Ingredients

1 cup Kosher salt

⅓ cup + 2½ Tbsp lemon pepper

¼ cup pepper

¼ cup Creole seasoning

¼ cup granulated garlic

5 tsp dried oregano

5 tsp dried basil

5 tsp dried marjoram

5 tsp dried thyme

5 tsp dried rosemary

¼ cup sugar

## Directions

• Mix all ingredients well and store in an airtight container.

 Tip from Chef "Wild" Bill:

Try it with extra virgin olive oil as an alternative to butter with Essential Baking Company Sourdough Bread. Unbelievable taste!

# BLACKENING SPICE OF LIFE gf

Many blackening spices are so hot that they literally burn up your mouth and leave you wondering whether there were any other flavors in the food you just ate. Here's a balanced approach that gives you some heat, but not so much that you can't enjoy the other delicate flavors in the dish. For a more modest experience, blacken only one side of the food.

Makes approximately 1 cup

## Ingredients

6 Tbsp kosher salt

½ cup paprika

3 Tbsp ground white pepper

3 Tbsp cayenne pepper

3 Tbsp sugar in the raw

3 Tbsp granulated garlic

2 Tbsp granulated onion

1 tsp dried thyme

1½ Tbsp ground black pepper

½ tsp dried basil

## Directions

• Mix all ingredients and store in an airtight container.

 Tip from Chef "Wild" Bill:

Cook blackened foods on a hot grill to caramelize the sugar and sear in the flavor.

# Forget Me Not

Don't forget about these recipes.

If you ignore them, you will probably regret it the rest of your life.

# DEGLAZING, DEMYSTIFIED BY CHEF "WILD" BILL

The deglazing process is a cooking technique that removes sediment left over from cooking an item. It lifts the remaining sauce in the pan and releases the flavor. It makes sauces or stocks taste more robust, and it can become the base for other sauces or broths. At Duke's, we use fish stock, liqueur or wine. (These last two will cause a flame so be careful.) To deglaze, first drain excess fat from the sauté pan while keeping the cooking seafood, meat or chicken in the pan. Then, stand back—here comes the flame (except for the non-alcoholic liquids) when you add your deglazing liquid. Then, swirl for ten seconds.

 Tip from Chef "Wild" Bill:

> Do not deglaze if the sediment is black. That means the ingredients were burned. It won't taste very good.

# INCREDIBLY HEALTHY VEGETABLE STOCK gf

Add nutrients and amazing flavor to any recipe that calls for water. You will be surprised by how much punch it adds to every dish.

Makes about 2 cups

| Ingredients | Directions |
|---|---|
| 1 cup celery, diced medium | • Heat Let's Be Clarified Butter in a soup pot. Add onion, celery, carrots and cook over high heat for 5 to 10 minutes, stirring frequently. |
| 1 cup onions, diced medium | |
| 1 cup carrots, diced medium | • Add salt and enough water to cover vegetables and bring to a boil. |
| 2 Tbsp Let's Be Clarified Butter (pg 148) | |
| ½ tsp sea salt | • Lower heat and simmer, uncovered, for 30 minutes. Strain, discarding the vegetables, and refrigerate. |

# HOW TO BOIL AN EGG

There are several ways to boil an egg. This one works well for us. Boil enough water to submerge all the eggs completely. Lightly salt the water. Once water is at a rolling boil, carefully place one egg at a time into the water. Boil for 11 minutes (over-cooking causes that "gray-edged" look). Remove pan from heat and run cold water over eggs for 2 minutes. Strain off the water to the level of the eggs and add ice (this completely stops the cooking process and will make the eggs very easy to peel) until the eggs are very cold. For a delicious spin that will become a party favorite, make your next batch of deviled eggs with fresh Dungeness Crab, a dash of Tabasco and fresh organic dill.

# ROASTED GARLIC CLOVES gf

- Shell and peel 1 pound fresh garlic cloves. Make sure hard tops are cut off. There should be no dark spots.

- Toss garlic in ¼ cup of extra virgin olive oil.

- Place garlic in a small baking dish and completely cover so no air escapes.

- Roast garlic until golden brown and cloves are soft to the touch.

- Cool in refrigerator.

 Tip from Chef "Wild" Bill:

- Strain the oil off the garlic cloves, and the next time you are using a recipe that calls for garlic and olive oil, use this oil. It's very flavorful, infused garlic olive oil, great for pasta dishes.

- After cooling, place oil and roasted garlic in blender and make roasted garlic paste. It is great as a healthy spread. Or add to mayo and make roasted garlic mayo. I've even made roasted garlic mustard by adding to Dijon.

# DUKE'S CRUNCHY CROUTONS

Makes 80 Croutons

## Ingredients

⅔ cup paprika

1 cup granulated garlic

½ cup onion powder

⅔ cup kosher salt

1 Tbsp dried basil

4 tsp dried parsley

1 Tbsp ground white pepper

1 - 6 oz Essential Baking Company Sourdough Bread (round loaf) or your favorite bread, cut in ¾ to 1-inch cubes

7 Tbsp Darigold butter, melted

## Directions

- Mix dry ingredients together.

- In large bowl, toss bread cubes with melted butter.

- Sprinkle with dry ingredients and toss until seasoning lightly covers each side of each crouton.

- Bake on a sheet pan at 350 degrees for 10 minutes.

# IT'S SOOO GOOD SEAFOOD STUFFING

This is an excellent all-around stuffing for seafood of all kinds. You can make a 4-ounce portion of Rockfish look enormous. If you were out on the water and didn't catch your limit, you'll stretch your catch and look like a hero at the dinner table.

Makes enough for approximately 8 fish stuffings

## Ingredients

4 oz fresh Dungeness Crabmeat

4 oz pre-cooked Wild Mexican Prawns (shells and tails removed and chopped fine)

6 Tbsp Havarti cheese, diced small

1 small sourdough dinner roll (about 1 oz), ground in a food processor

¼ cup grated Parmesan cheese

¼ cup grated Asiago cheese

¼ cup panko breadcrumbs (available at most grocery stores)

2 Tbsp green onion, green parts only, diced small

1 cup Make It Yourself Mayo (pg 320) or buy one made with olive oil

juice from one lemon

small pinch of white pepper

## Directions

• Mix all ingredients together in a bowl and refrigerate.

# SUNDRIED TOMATO RELISH gf

## Ingredients

1 cup oil-packed sun-dried tomatoes, drained and minced (we use local Tillen Farms)

3 Roasted Garlic Cloves (pg 328), minced

1 Tbsp lemon zest (very thin, small pieces)

¼ cup fresh organic parsley, diced small

½ cup fresh organic basil leaves, minced

¼ cup extra virgin olive oil

2 Tbsp honey

juice of 1 lemon

## Directions

• Mix all ingredients and refrigerate.

 Tip from Chef "Wild" Bill:

This recipe also works great on Halibut or any bottom fish, too. Try it with honey from different sources. Each region's honey has a distinct flavor that comes from the flowers nearby. Some farmers markets offer "tasters" so you can sample the differences between the different honeys. Dr. Brad Weeks makes honey on Whidbey Island, and it is simply exceptional.

# Baja Bandito Flour

This is a light breading recipe for any seafood dish. Not unlike a bandit, it steals the flavor for you without getting caught with the heavy feeling in the tummy.

## Ingredients

1 cup flour or Duke's Gluten-Free Flour Blend (pg 174)

1 tsp celery salt

½ tsp paprika

1 tsp kosher salt

1 tsp onion powder

1 tsp granulated garlic

½ tsp cayenne pepper

1 tsp white pepper

1 cup corn flour (we use Maseca Masa)

## Directions

- Whisk ingredients together in a mixing bowl. Store in an airtight container.

 Tip from Chef "Wild" Bill:

This breading is very light and can be used on just about any seafood if you are looking for a little crunch. There is nothing heavy here.

# "In Your Cups" Parmesan Cup gf

Add 2 Tbsp fresh grated Parmesan to a pre-heated flat griddle or unscratched pan. Melt completely. Then, while formed and still elastic, flip and melt another minute. Flip onto a coffee cup and mold into a cup shape. As it cools, it will harden into an edible "cheese cup."

# AVOCADO TOWER SALAD gf

## Ingredients

½ fresh avocado, diced medium

2 Tbsp Dukecumber Pico de Gallo (pg 275)

juice from half of a lime

1 tsp extra virgin olive oil

pinch Duke's Ready Anytime Seasoning (pg 323)

½ tsp Duke's Superb Herb Blend (pg 322)

## Directions

• Gently combine ingredients, (do not over-mix or avocado will turn to mush.) Place in a stainless steel tower mold (approximately 2-inch by 2-inch by 2-inch cube); then release on plate.

# "GIVE ME MORE TARTAR SAUCE" gf

This request is something we hear often at Duke's after people taste our tartar sauce. It seems simple to make, but most tartar sauces are surprisingly mundane. Capers are the key ingredient; they balance the sauce for the right amount of tart and sweet.

Makes 8-10 servings for two 3 oz. portions of fish

## Ingredients

2½ cups Make It Yourself Mayo (pg 320) or buy one made with olive oil

½ cup dill pickle relish (we use local Pleasant Valley)

6 Tbsp fresh Walla Walla Sweet onion, diced

2 Tbsp fresh squeezed lemon juice

1½ Tbsp Italian or Spanish capers

1½ Tbsp white pepper

2 Tbsp parsley, stems removed

1½ tsp Lea & Perrins Worcestershire Sauce

2 Tbsp fresh organic dill, stems removed

## Directions

• In a food processor, blend everything except for the mayonnaise thoroughly.

• Hand-mix mayonnaise until evenly incorporated. Keep chilled. Mayonnaise keeps for up to two weeks in the refrigerator.

# Forbidden Treats

You are in a safe
sweet zone.

# WHAT'S HER NAME'S CARROT CAKE gf

My favorite cake has always been carrot cake. Our Marketing Director, Bettina Carey, had a great recipe from a friend of hers. I could never remember her name, thus the name "What's Her Name" seemed appropriate. My mom always made the best frosting, so we used her technique in a collaborative effort, added some all-natural orange flavor and voila, What's Her Name's Carrot Cake was born. One of our guests told us that eating this dessert was like "angels dancing across your tongue."

Makes nine large cupcakes

## Dry Ingredients

2 cups flour or Gluten-Free Baker's Flour Blend (below)

2 tsp cinnamon

2 tsp baking powder

1½ tsp baking soda

¼ tsp ground nutmeg

pinch of ground cloves

1 tsp salt

## Wet Ingredients

¼ cup Woodford Reserve Bourbon (save a few sips for the baker)

1 tsp vanilla

1½ cups GMO-free canola oil

2 cups sugar

4 cage-free eggs

## Directions

• Sift dry ingredients and set aside.

• Blend wet ingredients well and add to dry ingredients.

• Add 2 cups grated carrots, 1½ cups crushed pineapple (well drained), ¾ cup chopped walnuts (optional).

• Mix until smooth and all ingredients are incorporated.

• Fill cupcake only halfway (leave enough room for cupcake to rise.) For large cupcakes, bake for 20-22 minutes. Cupcakes are done when toothpick inserted comes out clean. Wait until cake is room temperature before frosting the cupcakes.

• Top with Duke's Mom's Cream Cheese Frosting and 3 Candy Dandy Orange Peels (pg 338).

## Gluten-Free Baker's Flour Blend

1 cup sweet white sorghum flour

1 cup white rice flour

¾ cup cornstarch or ½ cup potato starch

1½ tsp xanthan gum (or guar gum)

½ tsp salt

• Sift and set aside.

## Duke's Mom's Cream Cheese Frosting

1 box powdered sugar (3 cups)

¼ lb Darigold butter, softened

8 oz cream cheese, softened

1 Tbsp vanilla

1 tsp all-natural orange extract

• Blend until smooth with no lumps.

# Duke's Grandfather's Chocolate Éclair

My grandfather started making Chowder 100 years ago in Fall River, Massachusetts. I wasn't really fond of Clams in my early days, but he had a great trick. He put chocolate éclairs in the middle of the table. If I didn't finish my Chowder, I didn't get a chocolate éclair. I loved those éclairs! At Duke's, our éclairs are made by Essential Baking Company here in Seattle. They are so decadent that your heart will skip a beat at the prospect of surrendering to the oh-my-goodness, from-the-heavens butter cream filling, rich in real butter and powdered sugar with just a hint of natural orange. Recipe compliments of Essential Baking Company.

Makes 24 Éclairs

## Pâte à Choux
### Ingredients

1 cup water

¼ lb Darigold butter

¾ tsp salt

½ cup flour

4 eggs

### Directions

- Sift the flour and set aside.

- Bring water, butter and salt to a boil in a large pot (leaving lots of room for the flour to be added).

- Keeping the liquid at a boil, slowly add the flour using a whisk. Once all of the flour is added, switch to a wooden spoon and stir constantly for approximately 3 minutes. When a film develops on the bottom of the pot the dough no longer sticks to it.

- Transfer dough to a stand mixer bowl. Using a paddle attachment, mix the dough on a low speed, letting it cool slightly, for approximately 5 minutes.

- Slowly add the eggs to the dough while the mixer is on a medium speed. Scrape down the sides of the bowl halfway through. Once all of the eggs have been added, check the dough's consistency by inserting the wooden spatula into the dough and pulling it straight up. The dough should hang off the spoon, forming a triangle shape. If the dough breaks off the spoon, then additional eggs are needed. Add one egg at a time and check consistency in between additions. If the dough forms a triangle, then it is ready to pipe.

- Using a large round tip fitted into a piping bag, pipe éclairs approximately 5.5" long.

- Bake éclairs in a convection oven at 350 degrees for 30 minutes; then reduce temperature to 325 degrees for 25 minutes.

- Before removing éclairs from the oven, break open an éclair to make sure there is a nice hollow pocket in its center. If a pocket has not formed yet, then bake for an additional 5 minutes.

- Let éclairs cool for approximately 1 hour.

## Naughty Orange Filling

### Ingredients

5 cups powdered sugar

¾ lb Darigold butter

3 cups cream cheese

2 Tbsp vanilla

3 Tbsp orange zest

### Directions

- Using a paddle attachment on a mixer, cream the butter and powdered sugar until light and fluffy. Slowly add chunks of the cream cheese on a medium speed, scraping down the sides of the bowl halfway through. Once all the cream cheese is added, slowly add the orange zest and vanilla. Scrape down the sides of the bowl halfway through.

- Using a medium size round tip fitted into a piping bag, pipe the icing into the éclairs until they are full.

- Let set in the refrigerator for approximately 2 hours.

## Charming Chocolate Glaze

### Ingredients

5 gelatin sheets

½ cup water

1 cup sugar

6 Tbsp and 1 tsp cocoa powder

6 Tbsp and 1 tsp Darigold cream

### Directions

- In a large pot, bring water and cream to a scald.

- Using a whisk, slowly add cocoa powder and sugar. Keep the liquid at a boil during addition of cocoa powder and sugar.

- Once all of the cocoa powder and sugar have been added, keep the glaze at a boil for an additional 2 minutes. Stir constantly with a whisk to ensure the glaze does not burn on the bottom of the pot.

- Remove from heat.

- Soak the gelatin sheets in cold water for about 3 minutes until they soften. Squeeze out excess water and add gelatin to the glaze. Stir until all gelatin is dissolved.

- Dip the top side of the filled éclair into the warm glaze. Shake off any excess glaze so it does not drip down the sides.

- Let the éclairs set in the fridge for an hour.

## Candy Dandy Orange Peel

### Ingredients

fresh orange peel

2 cups of simple syrup (pg 372)

### Directions

- Using only the orange-colored outside, slice orange peel as thinly as possible into 1-inch lengths.

- Boil 2 cups of simple syrup.

- Add orange peel and boil for 7 minutes.

- Using a slotted spoon, remove peel and place on a sheet pan lined with parchment paper. Spread and chill in the refrigerator. Top éclair with 3 Candy Dandy Orange Peels.

*The Woodford Reserve
trademark appears courtesy of
Brown-Forman Corporation.*

# "I WANT YOU SO BAD" MARIONBERRY PIE

This dessert has always been the favorite in the restaurant. Who doesn't love homemade pie? It's my favorite berry pie. Essential Baking Company now makes our recipe and, frankly, its bakers make it better than we do. They're bakers; we're cooks. Leave it to the experts.

This recipe is broken down from a larger recipe used by Essential Baking Company. It was a challenge to convert. It is worth the effort to make it, though. It's fabulous, especially with local ice cream from Lopez Island Creamery. It's a Little Taste Of Heaven.

Makes five 5-inch pies

## FLAKY NOT FAKY PIE DOUGH

| Ingredients | Directions |
| --- | --- |
| ½ cup + 3 Tbsp all purpose flour | • Mix dry ingredients together. |
| ¼ cup + 1 Tbsp organic pastry flour | • Add shortening in small chunks slowly. |
| ½ cup + 3 Tbsp shortening | • Add cold water in small additions. Do not over-mix. |
| ¼ cup + 3 Tbsp cold water | • Form dough in 5-inch pie pans. |
| 1 Tbsp granulated sugar | • Add filling and top with streusel. |
| 1 tsp salt | • Bake at 350 degrees for 16 minutes. |

## SHE'S SO BAD MARIONBERRY FILLING

| Ingredients | Directions |
| --- | --- |
| 1½ cups + 3 Tbsp raspberry jam | • Add jam to mixer with whip attachment. |
| 3 Tbsp + 1 tsp cornstarch | • Sprinkle cornstarch in while mixer is on lowest speed. |
| 2 cups marionberries | • Add water and lemon juice; mix until smooth. |
| 2 tsp water | • Add marionberries at end; mix in gently by hand. |
| 1 Tbsp lemon juice | |

# BEGUILING STREUSEL TOPPING

## Ingredients

½ cup all purpose flour

¼ cup + 2 tsp brown sugar

¼ cup + 1 Tbsp granulated sugar

pinch salt

pinch cinnamon

¼ cup + 2 tsp Darigold butter

## Directions

- Mix dry ingredients with paddle attachment.

- Add butter; mix until crumbly but dry.

## A Little Indulgence Is Good For You

Finding ice cream with no high fructose corn syrup wasn't easy. Alex Thieman, owner of local ice cream maker Lopez Island Creamery, was in the right place at the right time. "Wild" Bill, my son John, John Thelen, and I inspected Alex's small factory. As Alex said, "They wanted to know how our ice cream was made, where we were sourcing our ingredients, and exactly what was in each flavor, and we were very proud to tell them. Duke and his team care deeply about what they are serving their customers."

We love working with Alex and his ice cream team at Lopez Island Creamery. They hand-make their ice cream and can turn on a dime and produce anything we want whenever we want. They are in tune with our need for all-natural ingredients and their service is superb.

# Duketails
# & Classic
# Cocktails

We take cocktails
to another level.

Some of our "Duketails" are muddled, some shaken, some on the rocks and others are served straight up. No matter what your choice, all are unique, handcrafted concoctions that you won't find anywhere else.

# DUKE'S FAMOUS BLOODY BLOODY MARY

A slanted highball is a classic drink made in a happy little slanted glass. Nothing about the slanted highball is normal, but it will bring a smile to your face. This is the #1 selling drink at Duke's. It's nearly a meal in itself.

## Ingredients

1½ oz Duke's Bloody Mary Infused Vodka (pg 348)

5 oz Bloody Mary Mix (below)

1 lime wedge

2 Salacious Sauteed Prawns (below)

1 olive

1 Tillen Farms asparagus spear

## Directions

- First, squeeze lime wedge into a 12-14 oz glass with a salted rim (below).

- Fill with ice and add Duke's Bloody Mary Infused Vodka. Top with Bloody Mary Mix.

- Garnish with a skewer of 2 sautéed Prawns and an olive. Drop in the asparagus spear.

**For Salted Rim:** Pour kosher salt on a small plate. Rub a lime wedge around the rim of the glass. Slowly rotate the rim of the glass in the salt to adhere it.

## BLOODY MARY MIX

Makes enough for 3 Bloody Bloody Marys

### Ingredients

1 oz Demitri's Bloody Mary Seasoning

2 cups tomato juice

### Directions

- Mix all ingredients.

## SALACIOUS SAUTÉED PRAWNS  gf

Makes 6 Prawns—enough for 3 Bloody Bloody Marys

### Ingredients

6 Wild Mexican Prawns

1 Tbsp extra virgin olive oil

½ tsp fresh garlic, diced small

pinch Duke's Ready Anytime Seasoning (pg 323)

1 tsp fresh organic herbs (rosemary, thyme, oregano, stems removed from each), mixed

### Directions

- In small sauté pan, heat olive oil and add Prawns and garlic.

- When Prawns are halfway done, about 2 minutes, add fresh herbs and continue cooking for 1 more minute or until Prawns have lost all translucency.

- Remove from heat and chill Prawns in the refrigerator.

# Duke's Bloody Mary Infused Vodka

This Duke's signature brings a spicy fresh flavor of peppers, lemon, lime, garlic and pepper to take your Bloody Mary up a notch. This fan favorite makes Duke's Bloody Mary quite possibly the best Bloody Mary in town.

## Ingredients

750 ml New Amsterdam Vodka (or your favorite brand)

½ roasted yellow pepper

½ roasted red pepper

½ lemon, sliced into ¼-inch wheels

½ lime, sliced into ¼-inch wheels

1 garlic bulb

¼ cup whole black peppercorns

## Directions

- Preheat oven to 375.

- Slice one yellow and one red pepper in half. Remove stems and seeds.

- Slice the tips off of a whole bulb of garlic and place bottom-side down on a square of foil. Drizzle a teaspoon of olive oil over exposed tips and wrap foil around bulb.

- Place peppers (skin side up) and foil-wrapped garlic on a foil-lined baking sheet and roast at 375 degrees.

- After 15 minutes, remove peppers and slice into quarters.

- Bake garlic for an additional 20 minutes (35 minutes total). Unwrap garlic and squeeze cloves into a large bowl.

- Add citrus slices, black peppercorns, roasted pepper slices and New Amsterdam Vodka (save the bottle). Cover and infuse for 2 days. Strain and discard solids. Using a funnel, return vodka-infused mixture to its bottle.

# Cucumber Mojito

This concoction is quite possibly the most refreshing summer drink on the planet. This cocktail was born after a visit to a restaurant in Marina Del Rey. A traditional Mojito is made with rum, but we discovered that it tastes even more divine when combined with the pure taste of our Duke's Cucumber Infused Vodka. Good friend and ardent Duke's supporter, Rich Carr, believes this drink can deliver him to Nirvana. He wants the drink named after him, he likes it that much. I believe he is about halfway toward his minimum required consumption quota to earn that status, but his prospects look good.

## Ingredients

1½ oz Duke's Cucumber Infused Vodka (below)

2 lime wedges

5 mint leaves

2 slices of cucumber

½ oz Duke's Pure Cane Sugar Syrup (pg 372)

splash of Duke's Sweet & Sour Mix - about ½ oz (pg 372)

splash of soda water (about ½ oz)

## Directions

- First, add limes, mint and 1 cucumber slice to a pint glass. Add crushed ice to fill it nearly to the top. Muddle lightly for ten seconds, being careful to extract the juice from the fruit and the oils from the mint. Over-muddling will create too much rind taste.

- Add Duke's Cucumber Infused Vodka, cane syrup and Duke's Sweet & Sour Mix.

- Shake using a shaker tin and strain into a martini glass with sugared rim (below).

- Top with a splash of soda water and garnish with the second cucumber slice.

**For Sugared Rim:** Pour sugar on a small plate. Rub a lime wedge around the rim of a martini glass. Next, holding the glass rim-side down, rotate the rim in the sugar to adhere.

# Duke's Cucumber Infused Vodka

Cool, clean and refreshing, Duke's Cucumber Infused Vodka is the perfect remedy to a hot summer day.

## Ingredients

750 ml New Amsterdam Vodka (or your favorite brand)

2 medium-sized cucumbers

## Directions

- Score cucumbers with a peeler, removing strips of the peel. Slice cucumbers into ¼ inch slices and place in a large bowl.

- Add 750 ml of New Amsterdam Vodka (save the bottle) and refrigerate for about 2-3 days.

- Remove cucumbers with a slotted spoon. Using a funnel, return vodka infused mixture to its bottle.

# Duke's Manhattan

Each year, my partner and son John Moscrip, our Director of Operations John Thelen, Executive Chef "Wild" Bill Ranniger and I go to Kentucky to blend our own bourbon. For this business trip, I really have to twist arms to get people on board. Well, not really. We create what I call a "candy store" version of bourbon that combines notes of vanilla, caramel, chocolate, coffee, butterscotch, orange blossom, maple syrup and apricot. Master Distiller Chris Morris guides us through the process, and the result is a unique flavor that you can only find at Duke's. One sip of this drink takes me right to the heart of Manhattan.

## Ingredients

2 oz Duke's Woodford Reserve Personal Selection Bourbon (or regular Woodford Reserve)

½ oz Stirrings Blood Orange Bitters

½ oz Martini and Rossi Sweet Vermouth

1 Tillen Farms Merry Maraschino Cherry

## Directions

- Fill a pint glass with ice. Add bourbon, bitters and vermouth, and shake using a shaker tin.

- Strain into a martini glass and garnish with the cherry.

LABROT & GRAHAM

OODFORD RESERVE

DISTILLER'S SELECT

*Personal Selection*

KENTUCKY STRAIGHT BOURBON

Duke's Personal Blend #6

1 LITER                              90.4 PROOF

*The Woodford Reserve trademark appears
courtesy of Brown-Forman Corporation.
Woodford Reserve is a registered trademark of
Brown-Forman Corporation.*

# YOUNG & OLD FASHIONED

The Old Fashioned has made its way back onto the scene so we thought it was time to pay homage to the youthful beginnings of this old favorite by adding a little extra combination of flavor. (The secret is in the cherries and the Orange Bitters.)

## Ingredients

2 oz Woodinville Rye Whiskey

2 Tillen Farms Merry Maraschino Cherries, stems removed

10 drops Sun Liquor Orange Bitters

¼ oz Duke's Pure Cane Sugar Syrup (pg 372)

small splash of water

½ orange wheel

## Directions

• In a 12 oz glass, add 1 cherry, and using a dropper, add 10 drops of Sun Liquor Orange Bitters.

• Gently and slowly mash the cherry and bitters with a muddler.

• Add Duke's Pure Cane Sugar Syrup and whiskey.

• Top with ice and a small splash (¼ oz) of water.

• Garnish with ½ orange wheel on the side of the glass and the second cherry.

# OH MAI TAI!

Our spin on the traditional Mai Tai. There's only one thing to say, "Oh Mai," as it takes your breath away.

## Ingredients

1¼ oz Mount Gay Black Barrel Rum

½ oz Cointreau

2 lime wedges

2 oz pineapple and 1 oz orange juice

Float ½ oz Meyers Dark Rum

Float ½ oz Torani Pomegranate Syrup

1 Tillen Farms Merry Maraschino Cherry

½ orange wheel

## Directions

- First, squeeze 2 lime wedges into an empty pint glass and then fill with ice.

- Add Meyers Dark Rum, Cointreau, pineapple juice and orange juice.

- Fill glass with more ice and float with Meyers Rum and Torani Pomegranate Syrup.

- Garnish with the cherry and ½ orange wheel on a pick.

# BLOOD ORANGE MARGARITA

An orangey twist on a favorite that is so refreshing, if you close your eyes, just for a minute, you'll think you're kicking back on the sandy beaches of Mexico.

## Ingredients

1½ oz Milagro Reposado Tequila

¾ oz Solerno Blood Orange Liqueur

1 lime wedge

½ orange wheel

1 oz Duke's Sweet & Sour Mix (pg 372)

¼ oz cranberry juice

1 dried blood orange disc

Kosher salt and red sugar, mixed

**For Salt/Red Sugared Rim:** Mix 2 parts kosher salt and 1 part red sugar on a small plate. Using a lime wedge, wet the entire rim of a pint glass. Then rotate the rim of the pint glass in the salt/sugar mix to adhere.

## Directions

• First, place lime wedge and orange slice in a pint glass and fill with crushed ice. Muddle lightly for 10 seconds.

• Add Milagro Reposado Tequila, Solerno Blood Orange Liqueur and Duke's Sweet & Sour Mix. Shake gently using a shaker tin and pour into a fresh pint glass rimmed with the salt/red sugar mix.

• Top with ice and cranberry juice. Garnish with a dried blood orange disc.

# BLUEBERRY LEMON DROP

This delightful cocktail is a magnificent combination of lemon, orange and blueberry. Refreshing and delightful on any hot day.

## Ingredients

1½ oz Smirnoff Blueberry Vodka

½ oz Triple Sec orange liqueur

1 lemon wedge

10 fresh blueberries

½ oz Duke's Pure Cane Sugar Syrup (pg 372)

¼ oz lemonade

### For Sugared Rim:
Pour sugar on a small plate. Rub a lemon wedge around the rim of a martini glass. Slowly rotate the rim of the glass in the sugar to adhere.

## Directions

• First, place lemon wedge and 7 blueberries in a pint glass. Fill with crushed ice and muddle lightly for 10 seconds.

• Add Smirnoff Blueberry Vodka, Triple Sec, pure cane syrup and lemonade. Shake gently using a shaker tin, and strain into a martini glass with a sugared rim.

• Garnish with 3 blueberries.

# ORANGE MOJITO

The traditional mojito is kind of like the tango. It begs for improvisation and variation. This is a sweet spin on the refreshing classic, and it adds sweet notes, complements of spiced rum and orange.

## Ingredients

1½ oz Sailor Jerry's Spiced Rum

3 half-orange wheels

3 mint leaves

½ oz Duke's Pure Cane Sugar Syrup (pg 372)

¼ oz Duke's Sweet & Sour Mix (pg 372)

1 oz club soda

### For Sugared Rim:
Pour sugar on a small plate. Rub half of an orange wheel around the rim of a martini glass. Next, slowly rotate the rim of the glass in the sugar to adhere.

## Directions

• First, add 2 half-orange wheels and 3 mint leaves to a pint glass. Fill with crushed ice and muddle lightly for 10 seconds to extract the juice from the fruit and the oils from the mint. Caution: Over-muddling will cause too much rind taste.

• Add Sailor Jerry's Spiced Rum, Duke's Pure Cane Sugar Syrup, and Duke's Sweet & Sour Mix. Shake gently using a shaker tin, and strain into a sugar-rimmed martini glass.

• Top with club soda.

• Garnish with ½ orange wheel on the side of the glass.

# TITO'S MOSCOW MULE

The infamous Moscow Mule pairs lime flavor with vodka and ginger for a refreshing fizzy treat.

## Ingredients

1½ oz Tito's Handmade Vodka

4 lime wedges

12 oz bottle Cock 'n Bull Ginger Beer

## Directions

- First, squeeze and drop 3 lime wedges into a 12-14 oz copper mug (preferably) or glass.

- Add Tito's Handmade Vodka and fill to top with ice.

- Fill with Cock 'n Bull Ginger Beer, and garnish with an additional lime squeeze.

# BELL HOP

This drink is at your service . . . named for the vodka (Belvedere) that we use in this tasty beverage. Your guests might just leave a big tip if you make them one—it's that good. You won't even have to dress up like a bellhop.

## Ingredients

1½ oz Belvedere Citrus Vodka

2 lime wedges

2 lemon wedges

¼ oz light agave nectar

1 oz club soda

1 oz all natural lemon-lime soda (purchase one with no high fructose corn syrup)

1 lemon twist

## Directions

- First, add lime and lemon wedges to a pint glass. Nearly fill the glass with crushed ice and muddle lightly for about 10 seconds to extract the juice.

- Add Belvedere Citrus Vodka and agave, and shake gently using a shaker tin. Strain into a new glass.

- Fill with ice. Top with club soda and lemon-lime soda, and garnish with a lemon twist.

# KILLER CHERRY MOJITO

Not unlike our "Killer Prawns," this drink is so good that our servers have only two words for it, "killer good."

## Ingredients

1½ oz Mount Gay Silver Rum

2 lime wedges

5 mint leaves

2 Tillen Farms Merry Maraschino Cherries

1 Tbsp Tillen Farms Merry Maraschino Cherry juice

¼ oz Duke's Sweet & Sour Mix (pg 372)

3 oz club soda

### For Sugared Rim:

Pour sugar on a small plate. Rub a lime wedge around the rim of a pint glass. Next, slowly rotate the rim of the glass in the sugar to adhere.

## Directions

• First, add 2 lime wedges, 5 mint leaves, 1 Maraschino cherry (stem removed) to a pint glass and fill with crushed ice. Muddle lightly for 10 seconds to extract the juice from the fruit and the oils from the mint. Caution:  Over-muddling will cause too much rind taste.

• Add Mount Gay Silver Rum, cherry juice, and Duke's Sweet & Sour Mix. Shake gently using a shaker tin, and strain into an ice-filled glass with a sugared rim.

• Top with club soda, and garnish with remaining cherry.

# KAMIKAZE

There is some mystery and controversy surrounding the genesis of this drink. I'd like to share a little of Duke's history that might make the case for our authorship. One year back in the late 1970s on December 7th, Pearl Harbor Day, Mark Kobayashi, one of our managers, dressed as a Kamikaze pilot and decorated the restaurant in bold Japanese war posters. (He really pushed it to the edge of politically correct.) We created this drink to accompany his celebration and named it after his Kamikaze outfit. Soon other restaurants around the country started serving it, too.

## Ingredients

4 lime wedges

1½ oz Tito's Handmade Vodka

½ oz Triple Sec orange liqueur

## Directions

- Add 3 limes to a pint glass and fill with crushed ice. Muddle lightly for 10 seconds. Caution: Over-muddling will cause too much rind taste.

- Add Tito's Handmade Vodka and Triple Sec. Shake gently using a shaker tin and strain into a martini glass.

- Garnish with lime wedge on the side of the glass.

# THE ART OF MUDDLING

The origin of muddling can be traced to the mortar and pestle used as far back as 35,000 B.C. The same primitive idea of taking a grain, seed, spice or herb and grinding it down to mix it more easily or to extract the flavor is used in the muddling of cocktails today. The process entails gently smashing herbs, fruit slices or sugar cubes with a flat-ended wood tool against the bottom of a shaker tin or pint glass. This releases the delicate oils or juices without the earthy herb or bitter rind taste.

# DUKE'S PURE CANE SUGAR SYRUP (SIMPLE SYRUP)

| Ingredients | Directions |
|---|---|
| 1 cup water<br><br>2 cups pure cane sugar | • Boil water in a small saucepan and stir in sugar until just dissolved.<br><br>• Remove from heat and allow syrup to cool. Store covered at room temperature. |

**Bartender tip:** For a shortcut, purchase simple syrup at your local grocery store. Duke's uses Torani.

# DUKE'S SWEET & SOUR MIX

The way to a perfect sweet and sour mix to make it fresh. It may be tempting to buy the premade stuff, but your taste buds will know the difference. Plus, read the labels of those store-bought mixes and you'll find a lot of ingredients you can't even pronounce.

| Ingredients | Directions |
|---|---|
| ½ cup fresh lemon juice<br><br>¼ cup fresh lime juice<br><br>½ cup Duke's Pure Cane Sugar Syrup (above)<br><br>¾ cup water | • Pour all ingredients into a pitcher and stir. Cover and refrigerate. |

# Book Duke, "The Legend Himself" & "Wild" Bill Ranniger To Entertain Your Group

Described by many as a man of passion, mischievous, lighthearted, endearing and genuinely a kindhearted being, Duke Moscrip is a legend in the Pacific Northwest. Walk into a Duke's location on any given day or night and you are likely to catch him tasting the next iteration of an existing dish or concocting a new one with Executive Chef "Wild" Bill Ranniger. Together they would be working hard to ensure that each dish that is served at Duke's six locations has intense flavor as well as health benefits.

If you happen to meet Duke, reach out and shake his hand. You'll be greeted with a big smile and a warm welcome. Strike up a conversation and you'll soon be hearing how he fell in love with being a restaurateur over 40 years ago. A few moments more and you'll soon be learning how his adventures (Duke Tales, as his adventures have come to be known) to personally source the finest ingredients on the planet find their way into his restaurants serving you what both Duke and "Wild" Bill consider to be both the tastiest and healthiest meals for you.

Together, these two "Food Dudes," as they call themselves, will share their passionate journey to source the best ingredients. Through all of Duke's and "Wild" Bill's talks there is a singular message: eat well and you may just live forever.

Invite Duke, the legend himself, along with "Wild" Bill Ranniger to entertain at your next event. Learn how their passion to source incredibly healthy and tasty food has resulted in the success of Duke's Chowder Houses, known simply as an iconic restaurant chain in the Pacific Northwest.

In their entertaining program, Duke and "Wild" Bill reveal secrets behind their recipes included in their new cookbook, *As Wild As It Gets …Duke's Secret Sustainable Seafood Recipes*. You'll learn about sustainable sourcing and how you can play a giant role as a consumer by eating sustainably sourced seafood.

To book Duke, "The Legend Himself" and "Wild" Bill to entertain your group, call Bettina Carey at: 206-283-8422, ext. 4 or email her at emailclub@dukeschowderhouse.com.

# INDEX

# Gluten-Free Recipes

Duke's has been developing gluten-free recipes for a good many years. Our gluten-free offerings are special because they are just as delicious as their gluten counterparts. There has been no compromise in any way. Ingredients are healthy and flavor is outstanding. We have spent years testing and researching until we found just the right combination of Duke deliciousness and all natural nutrition. We hope you enjoy.

## Chowder Futures

Duke, Ian Jefferds of Penn Cove
Shellfish and "Wild" Bill

# Copyright, Photo Credits & Thank You!

There were many who contributed to the making of this book. Principal photography was provided by Ingrid Pape-Sheldon. We would like to thank Ingrid for her masterful photography which brought to life our story as well as acknowledge several others who contributed copy, photographs and/or illustrations to round out Duke's journey and history. Thank you one and all!

**Principal Photography** Ingrid Pape-Sheldon
Pages: 2, 4-5, 8-9, 10-11 (all five), 12-13, 14, 15, 18-19, 21 (all three), 22-23, 25, 26, 27, 28, 34 (all three), 35, 36-37, 38-39, 41, 43, 44-45, 46-47, 52 (far left), 53 (far right), 59 (far right) 61, 73, 77, 81, 82-83, 85, 87, 89, 91, 93, 95, 97, 99, 101, 103, 105, 107, 109, 111, 113, 115, 117, 119, 121, 123, 125, 127, 129, 130-131, 133, 141, 143, 145, 153, 154-155, 157, 159, 161, 163, 165, 167, 169, 171, 175 (all three), 178-179, 181, 185, 187, 189, 191, 193, 195, 197, 199, 201, 203, 205, 207, 209, 213, 217, 219, 221, 223, 225, 227, 229, 231, 233, 236, 239, 241, 243, 245, 247, 249, 251, 253, 255, 257, 263, 265, 267, 269, 271, 273, 277, 281, 283, 285, 289, 291, 295, 296-297, 299, 301, 303, 305, 307, 309, 311, 313, 315, 317, 319, 325, 327, 333, 335, 337, 340-341, 345, 347, 349, 351, 353, 355, 357, 359, 361, 363, 365, 367, 369, 371, 373, 383 (bottom right). Cover photos and author's photographs.

## Producer & Art Director
Bettina Carey, Marketing Director
Author & Photographer Pages Dust cover (left panel), 58 (second from left), 334 (co-author of recipe) 339, 373, 374-380, 381 (bottom), 383 (top right & bottom left)

## Book Design
Aileen Yost, Design Director
Cover Design, Co-Design Book Interior, DukeWorthy™ Stamp, 13th Man Ad Page 68

Suzanne Harkness, Graphic Designer & Illustrator
Co-Design Book Interior, Technical Layout Designer
Illustrations Pages 56, 74-75

## Other Contributors
Bruce Bailey, Photographer & Illustrator Pages 176, 381 (top)
Georgio Brown, Videographer & Photographer Pages 49, 51 (middle left, bottom left, bottom right), 53 (left), 54, 55, 235 (top)
Rich Carr, Photographer Page 6
Paulo Coehlo, Quote Page 13
Clay Eals, Photographer Pages 59 (left), 383 (top left)
Fish2Fork, Logo Page 53
Jeff Hobson, Photographer Pages 66, 240
Larry Liffick, Photographer Page 63
Karina Medina, Photographer Page 383 (center)
Bob Peterson, Photographer Pages 66, 177, 211, 261, 293
Roddy Scheer, Videographer & Photographer Pages 48 (right), 52 (second from left)
Bob Simon, Photographer Pages 48 (left), 51 (top left) 57, 148, 384
SmartCatch, Logo Page 53
Julie Sparrowgrove, Photographer Page 65
Amy Waeschle, Pages 29, 62, Duke & Bill's Bio (dust cover)
Dr. Bradford S. Weeks, M.D., N.D. Pages 76, 78-79

Woodford Reserve Trademark Appears Courtesy of Brown-Forman Corporation Pages 339, 353

In addition, we'd like to thank and acknowledge our DukeWorthy™ providers who provided their logos, their stories about working with us and in some cases photos.

## DukeWorthy™ Providers
Ameristar Meats, Page 292
Alaska Seafood Marketing Institute, Page 183
Alaska Weathervane Scallops, Page 234, 235 (bottom, Chris Miller, Photographer)
Aqua Star, Page 244
Chris Produce Co. Inc., Page 116
Cuizina Food Company, Page 173
Darigold, Pages 150-151
Food Services of America, Page 292
Harvestland/Perdue, Page 290
Heinz, Page 300
Lopez Island Creamery, Page 343
Penn Cove Shellfish, LLC, Page 98
Meridian, Page 94
Pacific Seafood, Page 215
Penny's Salsa and Fresh Produce, Page 275
Sea Watch International, Page 174
Service Linen Supply, Page 172
Simplot, Page 300
The Essential Baking Company, Pages 142, 143 (Recipe), 336
Tillamook, Page 296
Trident Seafood, Page 260
Yakutat Seafoods, Page 210

*Above:* Videographer Georgio Brown and Photographer Ingrid Pape-Sheldon documenting the evolution of Duke's brand. Be sure to check out all of the Duke Tales videos on our YouTube channel.

The "cookbook crew" hard at work. *Above from left:* Designer Suzanne Harkness, Design Director Aileen Yost, Duke, Principal Photographer Ingrid Pape-Sheldon, Marketing Director Bettina Carey and Bob Bracht of Colorgraphics.

At Duke's, it is never goodbye.
It is always the beginning of a great meal, a great relationship and great friends.
We will see you again.

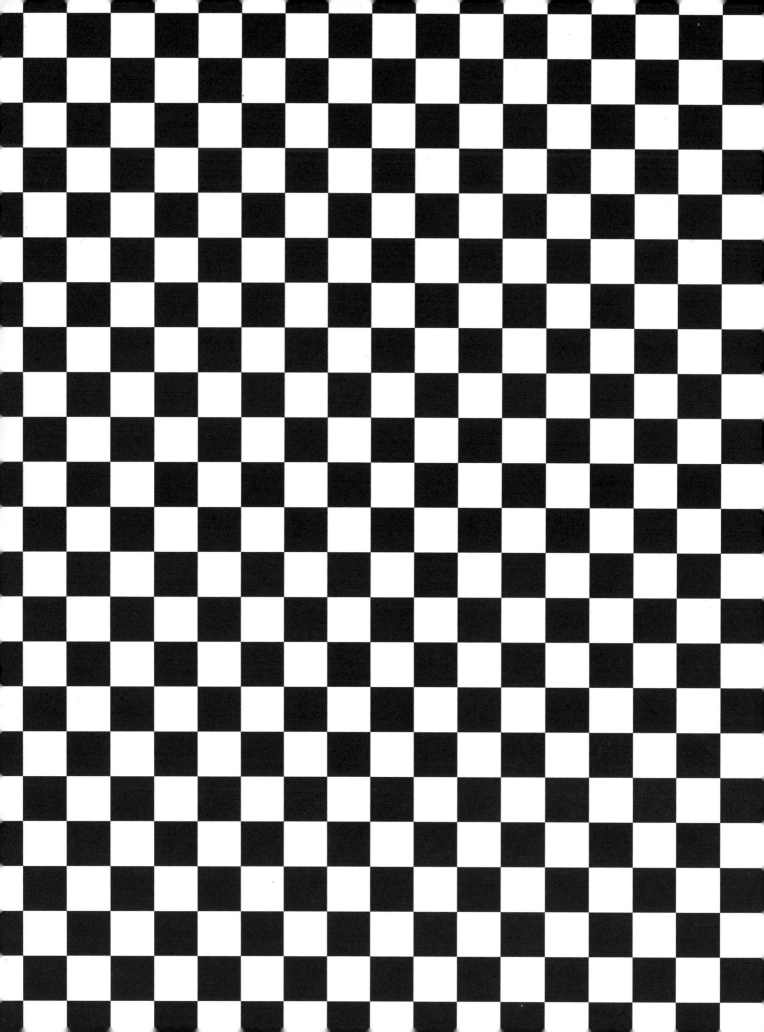